Answers to Revision Questions for National 5 Physics

Campbell White

Formerly Principal Teacher of Physics
Tynecastle High School, Edinburgh

Published by
Chemcord
Inch Keith
East Kilbride
Glasgow

ISBN 9781870570275

© White, 2016

All rights reserved. No part of this publication may be reproduced or transmitted in any form or by any means, electronic or mechanical, including photocopy, recording, or any information storage and retrieval system, without permission in writing from the publisher or under licence from the Copyright Licensing Agency.

Printed by Bell and Bain Ltd, Glasgow

Contents

Unit 1	Electricity and Energy	
	Conservation of energy	1
	Electrical charge carriers and electric fields	4
	Potential difference (voltage)	8
	Ohm's law	9
	Practical electrical and electronic circuits	13
	Electrical power	26
	Specific heat capacity	31
	Gas laws and the kinetic model	35
Unit 2	Waves and Radiation	
	Wave parameters and behaviours	44
	Electromagnetic spectrum	50
	Light	54
	Nuclear radiation	56
Unit 3	Dynamics and Space	
	Velocity and displacement – vectors and scalars	67
	Acceleration	73
	Velocity-time graphs	75
	Newton's laws	78
	Projectile motion	90
	Space exploration	92
	Cosmology	100

Open-ended Questions		**103**
Model answers to Open-ended Questions		**104**

Unit 1   Electricity and Energy

Conservation of energy

Energy transfer and conservation

1. (a) E (b) the joule, J

2. (a) chemical   (b) kinetic   (c) potential   (d) heat

3. the change in energy from one form to another

4. (a) The chemical energy associated with its fuel is transformed into kinetic energy.
   (b) Kinetic energy is transformed into heat energy in the brakes.
   (c) Chemical energy is transformed into potential energy.
   (d) Potential energy is transformed into heat energy in the brakes.

5. (a) not wasting energy
   (b) Most of our energy needs at present come from fossil fuels and these sources are finite.

6. (a) insulating the home; turning off lights when leaving a room; turning down the temperature at the thermostat; switching off appliances when not in use
   (b) carrying more people per vehicle; not making unnecessary journeys; using public transport more often; using rail rather than roads for carrying goods

7. Energy can be transformed from one type to another, but it can neither be created nor destroyed.

8. Energy **cannot** be lost; the ball loses potential energy but this is transformed into other types of energy, mainly kinetic energy.

Potential and kinetic energy

1. (a) $E_p = mgh$

   (b) and (c)
   E_p is gravitational potential energy which is measured in joules, J
   m is mass which is measured in kilograms, kg
   g is gravitational field strength (or acceleration due to gravity) which is measured in newtons per kilogram, N kg^{-1}
   (or is measured in metres per second per second, m s^{-2})
   h is vertical distance (height) which is measured in metres, m

2. mass, $m = 52$ kg
   height, $h = 1.5$ m
   $g = 9.8$ m s^{-2} (not stated explicitly)
   $E_p = mgh = 52 \times 9.8 \times 1.5 = 764.4$ J   (760 J to 2 significant figures)

3. mass, $m = 105$ kg
   height, $h = 250 - 75 = 175$ m
   $g = 9.8$ m s^{-2} (not stated explicitly)
   $E_p = mgh = 105 \times 9.8 \times 175 = 180\,075$ J
                        (180 000 J, or 180 kJ to 2 significant figures)

4. mass of water per second, $m = 4$ tonnes $= 4 \times 1000$ kg
   height, $h = 50$ m
   $g = 9.8$ m s^{-2} (not stated explicitly)
   energy available every second   = mgh
                                   = $4 \times 1000 \times 9.8 \times 50$
                                   = 1.96×10^6 J
                        (2×10^6 J, or 2 MJ to 1 significant figure)

5. kinetic energy

6. The greater the **mass** and/or the greater the **speed** of a moving object, the greater is its kinetic energy.

7. (a) $E_k = \tfrac{1}{2}mv^2$

   (b) E_k is kinetic energy measured in joules, J
   m is mass measured in kilograms, kg
   v is speed measured in metres per second, m s^{-1}

8. mass, $m = 0.75$ kg
    speed, $v = 2.0$ m s^{-1}
    $E_k = \tfrac{1}{2}mv^2$
    $= \tfrac{1}{2} \times 0.75 \times 2.0^2 = 1.5$ J

9. Car:
    mass, $m = 800$ kg
    speed, $v = 26$ m s^{-1}
    $E_k = \tfrac{1}{2}mv^2$
    $= \tfrac{1}{2} \times 800 \times 26^2 = 270\,400$ J

    Lorry:
    mass, $m = 3000$ kg
    speed, $v = 13$ m s^{-1}
    $E_k = \tfrac{1}{2}mv^2$
    $= \tfrac{1}{2} \times 3000 \times 13^2 = 253\,500$ J

    The car has the greater kinetic energy.

10. mass, $m = 38$ kg
    height, $h = 5.0$ m
    speed $= 5.5$ m s^{-1}
    $g = 9.8$ m s^{-2} (not stated explicitly)
    $E_p = mgh = 38 \times 9.8 \times 5.5 = 1862$ J
    $E_k = \tfrac{1}{2}mv^2 = \tfrac{1}{2} \times 38 \times 5.5^2 = 574.75$ J

    energy transferred by friction $= (1862 - 574.75)$
    $= 1287.25$ J   (1300 J to 2 significant figures)

11. All of the potential energy of an object ($E_p = mgh$) is transformed into kinetic energy ($E_k = \tfrac{1}{2}mv^2$) when it falls.
    so $E_p = E_k$
    so $mgh = \tfrac{1}{2}mv^2$
    but since the mass is the same, $gh = \tfrac{1}{2}v^2$
    so $v^2 = 2gh$
    so $v = \sqrt{2gh}$

    g is constant, so speed depends only on height

12. height, $h = 80$ m
    $g = 9.8$ m s^{-2} (not stated explicitly)

    (a) E_k at bottom $= E_p$ at top
        so $v = \sqrt{2gh} = \sqrt{2 \times 9.8 \times 80} = 39.6$ m s^{-1} (40 ms^{-1} to 2 significant figures)

    (b) It will be less than 40 ms^{-1} since not all of the potential energy will be transformed into kinetic energy.

    (c) heat

Electrical charge carriers and electric fields

Electrical charge and electrical current

1. An electrical conductor contains charged particles that can move and allow an electric current. The charges in an insulator are not free to move.

2. (a) metals; graphite; water
   (b) e.g. plastics; wood; glass; paper

3. positive and negative

4. Most materials are made up of atoms that contain equal numbers of positively and negatively charged particles.

5. (a) Rub the rod with a cloth.
   (b) The cloth gains negatively charged particles. The rod becomes positive as it has lost negatively charged particles.

6. (a) unlike charges attract
   (b) like charges repel

7. negative charge

8. (a) Q (b) the coulomb, C

9. the rate of flow of charges, usually negative charges carried by electrons, in a conductor

10. (a) I (b) the ampere, A

11. $Q = It$

12. charge, $Q = 180$ C
    time, $t = 1$ minute $= 60$ s
    $Q = It$ ∴ $180 = I \times 60$ so $I = \dfrac{180}{60} = 3 \text{ A}$

13. current, $I = 0.25$ A
    time, $t = 1$ hour $= 60 \times 60$ s $= 3600$ s
    $Q = It = 0.25 \times 3600 = 900$ C

14. charge, $Q = 20$ mC $= 20 \times 10^{-3}$ C
 current, $I = 0.5$ μA $= 0.5 \times 10^{-6}$ A

 $Q = It$ ∴ $20 \times 10^{-3} = 0.5 \times 10^{-6} \times t$
 so $t = \dfrac{20 \times 10^{-3}}{0.5 \times 10^{-6}} = 4 \times 10^{4}$ s

Alternating and direct current

1. (a) the type of current where the charges go backwards and forwards many times a second

    (b) the type of current where the charges flow the same way all the time

2. to provide a source of electrical energy

3. (a) a.c.   (b) d.c.

4. (a) a.c. from the mains   (b) d.c. from a battery

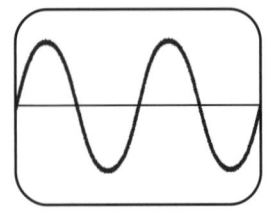

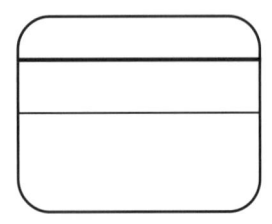

Electric fields

1. The region around an electric charge where it can affect another charge is said to have an electric field acting on it.

2. Charges experience a force when they are in an electric field.

3. (a) Electric fields can be represented by drawing field lines.

    (b) An electric field is strongest where the field lines are closest together.

    (c) (i) The direction of an electric field is conventionally represented by arrowheads.

    (ii) The arrowheads point in the direction that a positive charge would move.

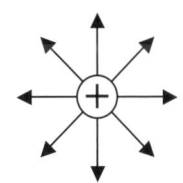

4. (a)   (b)   radial field

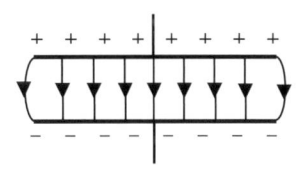

5. (a)   (b)   uniform field

6. Free electric charges in a conductor move.

7. (a) The charged particle is accelerated by the force due to the field.

    (b) The charged particle follows a parabolic path in the electric field.

Potential difference (voltage)

1. a measure of the energy given to the charges in a circuit

2. (a) V (b) the volt, V

3. The brightness of a lamp increases.

4. Voltage is a measure of the amount of energy given to the charges in a circuit. Current is a measure of the rate at which charges flow round a circuit. The voltage applied to a circuit causes the charges in the circuit to flow and this flow of charges is the current.

Ohm's law

Resistance

1. a measure of the opposition to the flow of charges

2. electrical energy to heat energy

3. (a) R (b) the ohm, Ω

4. The current decreases.

5. (a) $R = \dfrac{V}{I}$

   (b) V is the potential difference (voltage) measured in volts, V
   I is the current measured in amperes, A
   R is the resistance measured in ohms, Ω

6.

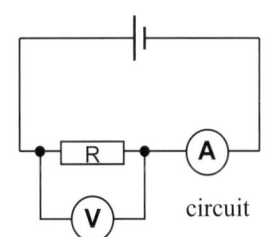

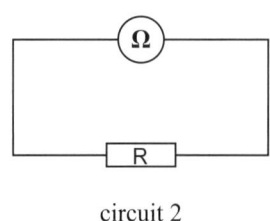

circuit 1   circuit 2

Use circuit 1 to measure the current I in and the voltage V across the resistor.
Use circuit 2 to measure the resistance R of the resistor.
Divide V by I to show that $R = \dfrac{V}{I}$.

7. (a) Change the resistance of the variable resistor and each time note the corresponding voltmeter and ammeter reading.

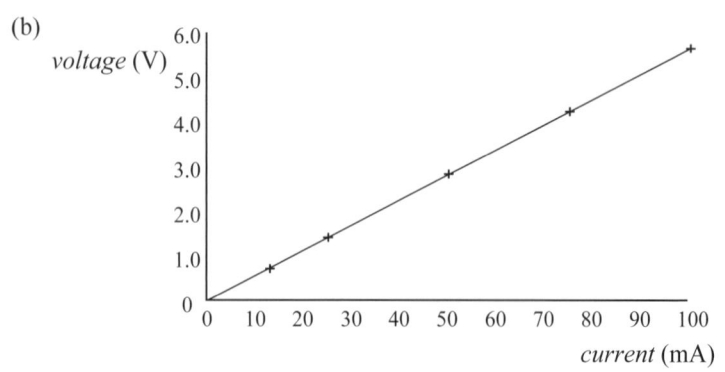

(b)

voltage (V) vs current (mA)

(c) any pair of values from the graph can be used, e.g.

$$R = \frac{V}{I} = \frac{5.6}{0.1} = 56\ \Omega$$

8. The current in a conductor at constant temperature is directly proportional to the voltage across it.

9. (a) resistance, which is a property of the resistor, not the current through it nor the voltage across it

    (b) The ratio remains approximately constant.

10. (a) one that obeys Ohm's law   (b) resistor; variable resistor

11. (a) one that does **not** obey Ohm's law, i.e. the ratio $\frac{V}{I}$ is **not** constant;

    (b) filament lamp; diode; thermistor; LDR; photovoltaic cell

12. As the temperature increases, the resistance of metallic conductors increases. Constantan is an alloy designed to have a resistance that does not vary as temperature changes. The resistance of graphite falls as the temperature increases.

Calculations

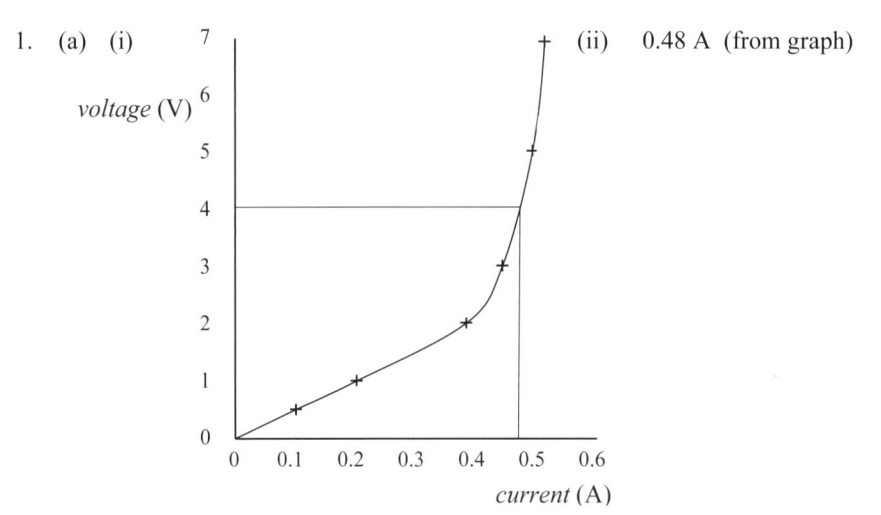

1. (a) (i)

(ii) 0.48 A (from graph)

(b) $R = \dfrac{V}{I}$

Reading on voltmeter (V)	Reading on ammeter (A)	Resistance of lamp (Ω)
0.5	0.10	5.0
1.0	0.20	5.0
2.0	0.38	5.3
3.0	0.44	6.8
5.0	0.49	10
7.0	0.51	14

(c) (i) The resistance of the lamp increases.

(ii) The filament heats up; the resistance increases with increasing temperature.

2. current, $I = 3$ A
   voltage, $V = 12$ V

$$R = \dfrac{V}{I} = \dfrac{12}{3} = 4 \text{ Ω}$$

3. voltage, $V = 9$ V
   resistance, $R = 180$ Ω

$$R = \dfrac{V}{I} \quad \therefore 180 = \dfrac{9}{I} \quad \text{so } I = \dfrac{9}{180} = 0.05 \text{ A, or 50 mA}$$

Electricity and Energy Answers

4. resistance, $R = 1\ \text{k}\Omega = 1000\ \Omega$
   current, $I = 10\ \text{mA} = 10 \times 10^{-3}\ \text{A}$

   $R = \dfrac{V}{I} \quad \therefore 1000 = \dfrac{V}{10 \times 10^{-3}} \quad \text{so } V = 10 \times 10^{-3} \times 1000 = 10\ \text{V}$

5. reading on voltmeter, $V = 9.0\ \text{V}$
   reading on ammeter, $I = 50\ \text{mA} = 0.05\ \text{A}$

   $R = \dfrac{V}{I} = \dfrac{9.0}{0.05} = 180\ \Omega$

Practical electrical and electronic circuits

Current, voltage and resistance in circuits

1. (a) (i) an ammeter (b) —(A)—
   (ii) a voltmeter —(V)—
   (iii) an ohmmeter —(Ω)—

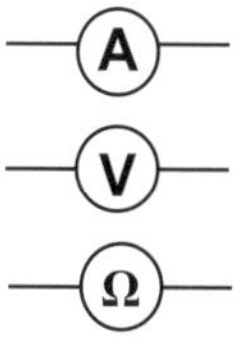

2. (a), 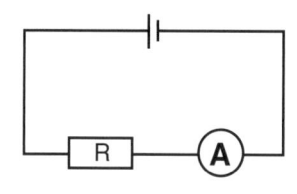 (b), 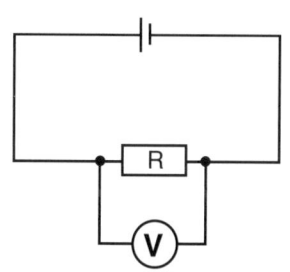 (c) [circuit diagrams]

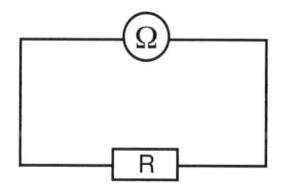

3. (a), 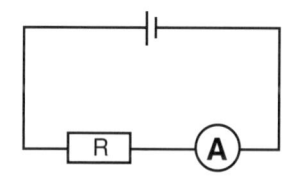 (b) [circuit diagrams]

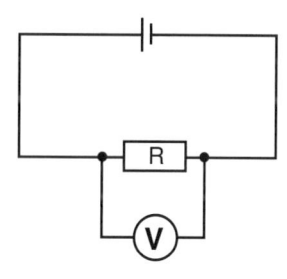

4. [circuit diagram]

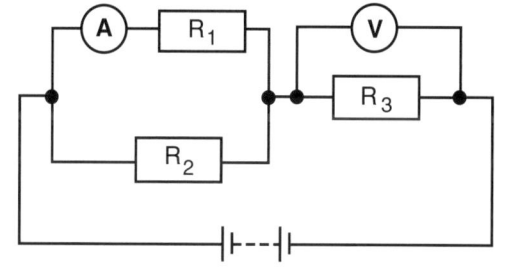

Electrical and electronic components

1. (a) and (b)
   - (i) a cell — source of energy;
   - (ii) a battery — source of energy;
   - (iii) a lamp — transformation of electrical energy into light energy;
   - (iv) a switch — makes and breaks the circuit;
   - (v) a resistor — opposes current;
   - (vi) a fuse — breaks circuit when current becomes too large.

2. (a) battery, switch, resistor
   (b) cell, fuse, lamp

3. (a) to alter the current in a circuit
   (b) [variable resistor symbol]
   (c) light dimmers; sewing machine speed controls; volume controls; computer joysticks

4. lamps and thermistors where the resistance changes as the temperature changes; light dependent resistors where the resistance changes as the light level changes

5. (a) transformation of electrical energy into kinetic energy
   (b) —(M)—

6. (a) an electronic device that allows current in one direction only
   (b) [diode symbol]

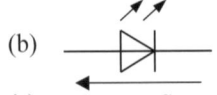

7. (a) light emitting diode
   (b) [LED symbol]
   (c) electron flow
   (d) low energy lighting, e.g. car brakelights

8. The LED will not emit light because it will not allow a current through.

9. An LED uses low values of current; the resistor protects the LED by ensuring that the current is not too high.

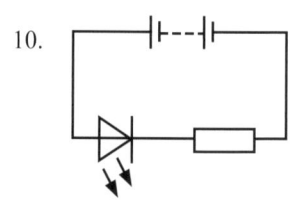

10. [circuit diagram]

11. voltage across resistor = 12 − 2 = 10 V
    current, $I = 10$ mA $= 10 \times 10^{-3}$ A
    $$R = \frac{V}{I} = \frac{10}{10 \times 10^{-3}} = 1000 \; \Omega$$

12. (a) [symbol]

    (b) sound energy to electrical energy

13. (a) [symbol]

    (b) electrical energy to sound energy

14. (a) [symbol]

    (b) light energy to electrical energy

    (c) e.g. power supplies for space craft; light meters

15. (a) a THERMal resISTOR

    (b) A thermistor has a resistance that changes as its temperature changes; normally the higher the temperature, the lower its resistance.

    (c) [symbol]

    (d) to measure temperature

16. resistance, $R = 30 \; \Omega$
    potential difference, $V = 9$ V
    $$R = \frac{V}{I} \quad \therefore 30 = \frac{9}{I} \quad \text{so } I = \frac{9}{30} = 0.3 \text{ A, or 300 mA}$$

Electricity and Energy Answers

17. (a) light dependent resistor
    (b) a resistor with a resistance that changes as the light level falling on it changes; normally the greater the light intensity, the lower its resistance.
    (c) [symbol]
    (d) e.g. as automatic light controls; light sensors in alarms such as burglar alarms

18. current, $I = 10$ mA $= 10 \times 10^{-3}$ A
    potential difference, $V = 4$ V
    $$R = \frac{V}{I} = \frac{4}{10 \times 10^{-3}} = 400 \, \Omega$$

19. (a) [symbol]
    (b) acts as a remote switch

20. (a) stores charge in an electronic circuit
    (b) [symbol]

21. (a) [circuit diagram]
    (b) The potential difference increases.
    (c) [graph of voltage (V) vs time (s) showing capacitor charging curve]

22. (a) when it is fully charged, at which time the voltage across it is equal to the supply voltage
    (b) the resistance of the series resistor, R, and the capacitance of the capacitor, C

Electricity and Energy Answers

23. by using a series resistor of lower resistance

24. by joining the two ends together with a piece of wire

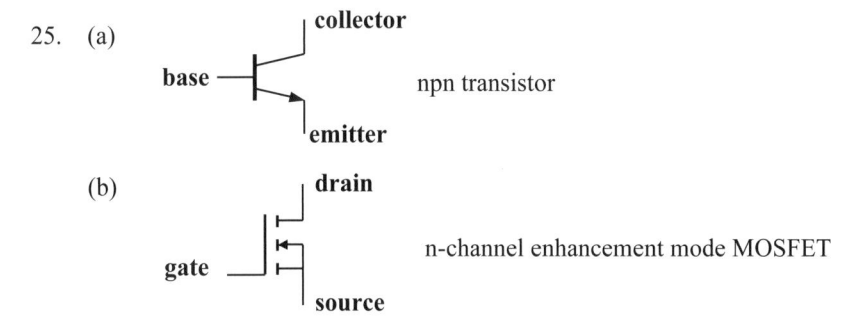

25. (a) npn transistor — with labels: collector, base, emitter

    (b) n-channel enhancement mode MOSFET — with labels: drain, gate, source

26. (a) e.g. as a switch

    (b) The transistor is OFF (non-conducting) until the input voltage is high enough, at which point the transistor switches ON (starts conducting).

Electricity and Energy Answers

Series and parallel circuits

1. (a) one where there is only one path for the charges to follow; all of the components are connected one after the other

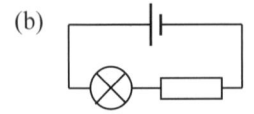

   (b) [circuit diagram: battery, bulb and resistor in series]

2. The current is the same at all points in a series circuit.

3. The sum of the voltages across the components in a series circuit is equal to the voltage of the supply.

4. All the energy given to the charges in the circuit by the supply is transferred to the series components and then the charges pass through the supply again to collect more energy.

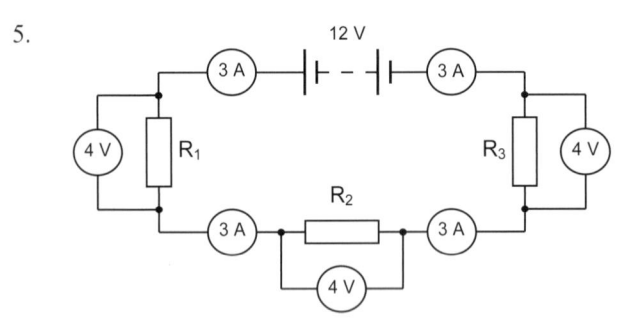

5. [circuit diagram: 12 V supply, currents of 3 A, resistors R_1, R_2, R_3 with voltages 4 V, 4 V, 4 V]

6. connecting any appliance that has its own switch to the mains by means of a switched socket

7. (a) one which has more than one branch or path for charges to follow

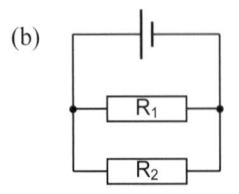

   (b) [circuit diagram: battery with R_1 and R_2 in parallel]

8. The current drawn from the supply in a parallel circuit is equal to the sum of the currents in the individual branches.

18 Electricity and Energy Answers

9. The voltage across each component in a parallel circuit is the same. If the components are connected directly across the supply, the voltage is also equal to the supply voltage.

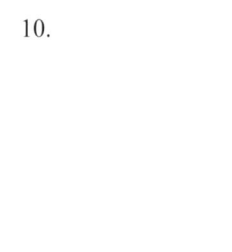

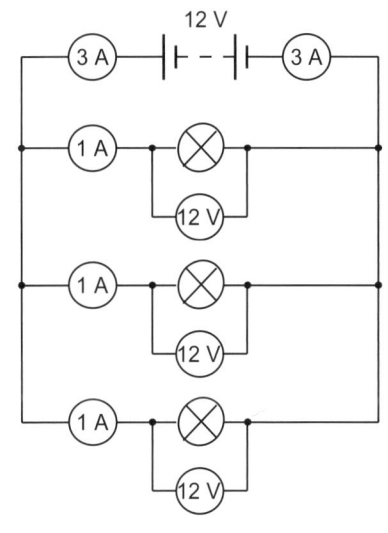

10.

11. A large current could be drawn from the supply and may cause the wiring or the socket to be overheated.

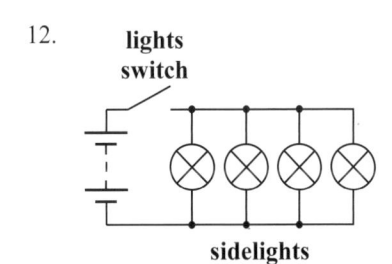

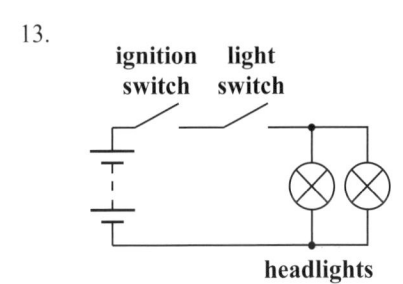

12.

13.

14.

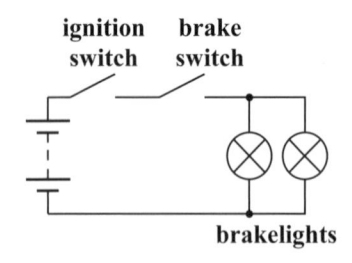

      ignition   brake
      switch   switch

(circuit diagram with battery, ignition switch and brake switch in series with two brakelights in parallel)

               brakelights

15. (a) The door switch closes.

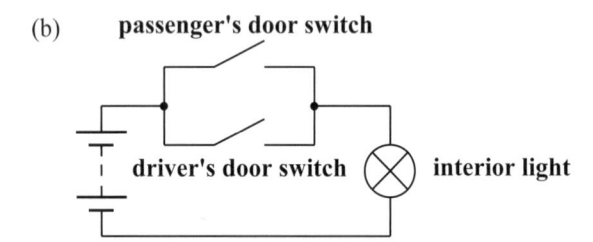

    (b) **passenger's door switch**

(circuit diagram showing driver's door switch and passenger's door switch in parallel, connected to interior light and battery)

        driver's door switch   interior light

16. (a) one where there is a break in the circuit

    (b) one where a component or components have the ends joined directly together by a conductor

17. (a) It can be made from a cell and a current indicator, such as a lamp, along with two probe wires.
The lamp lights up when the probes are connected by a conductor.

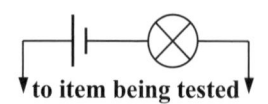

(circuit diagram: cell, lamp, and two probes labelled "to item being tested")

    (b) When a continuity tester is connected across an open circuit, the lamp does not light. When connected across a short circuit, the lamp lights brightly.

18. (a) infinite resistance

    (b) zero resistance

19. (a) in parallel

    (b) a parallel circuit

20. (a) a parallel circuit in house wiring used for the power sockets; the live, neutral and earth wires start at the consumer unit, go to all of the sockets on the ring main and return to the consumer unit, forming a large loop

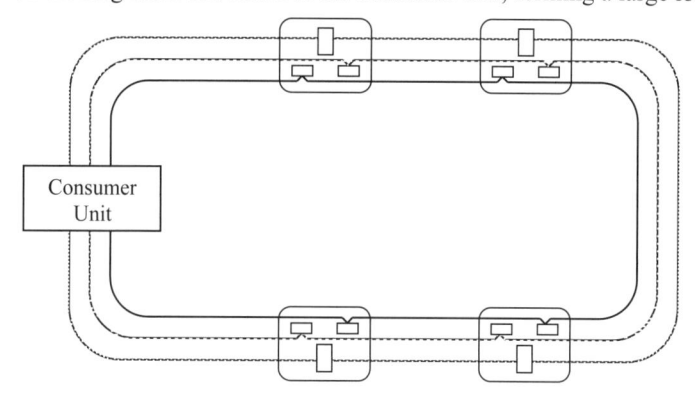

(b) Since there are two paths for the current to follow to each socket, the cables used can be smaller and therefore cheaper; there is less current in each part of the cable; a ring main circuit is more convenient since sockets can be placed anywhere on the ring.

(c) The lighting circuit supplies the fixed lights in the house, the ring main circuit supplies the power sockets; the lighting circuit is a 5 A circuit, the ring main circuit is a 30 A circuit; the lighting circuit uses smaller cable than the ring main circuit; the lighting circuit is a parallel circuit, the ring main circuit is a loop parallel circuit.

21. (a) to protect the mains wiring of a house

(b) A mains fuse is made of thin wire which heats up and melts if the current drawn from the circuit becomes too great. In this way the mains wiring of the house is protected because the current is cut off.

22. (a) Each circuit needs its own mains fuse.

(b) Each circuit is designed for different maximum currents:
a 5 A fuse is used for each lighting circuit;
a 15 A fuse is used for an immersion heater circuit;
a 30 A fuse is used for each ring main circuit.

Resistors in circuits

1. (a) ─[R₁]─[R₂]─[R₃]─

   (b) $R_T = R_1 + R_2 + R_3$

   (c) The total resistance increases.

2. (a) $R_T = R_1 + R_2 = 82 + 18 = 100 \; \Omega$

   (b) $R_T = R_1 + R_2 + R_3 = 56.0 + 22.0 + 47.0 = 125 \; \Omega$

3. $R_T = R_1 + R_2 + R_3 = 2.20 + 4.70 + 5.60 = 12.5 \; \Omega$

4. (a) [R₁, R₂, R₃ in parallel]

   (b) $\dfrac{1}{R_T} = \dfrac{1}{R_1} + \dfrac{1}{R_2} + \dfrac{1}{R_3}$

   (c) The total resistance decreases.

5. (a) $\dfrac{1}{R_T} = \dfrac{1}{R_1} + \dfrac{1}{R_2} = \dfrac{1}{12} + \dfrac{1}{15} = \dfrac{5+4}{60} = \dfrac{9}{60}$ so $R_T = \dfrac{60}{9} = 6.7 \; \Omega$

   (b) $\dfrac{1}{R_T} = \dfrac{1}{R_1} + \dfrac{1}{R_2} + \dfrac{1}{R_3} = \dfrac{1}{2.00} + \dfrac{1}{5.00} + \dfrac{1}{10.0} = \dfrac{5+2+1}{10} = \dfrac{8}{10}$ so $R_T = \dfrac{10}{8} = 1.25 \; \Omega$

6. $\dfrac{1}{R_T} = \dfrac{1}{R_1} + \dfrac{1}{R_2} + \dfrac{1}{R_3} = \dfrac{1}{10} + \dfrac{1}{12} + \dfrac{1}{15} = \dfrac{6+5+4}{60} = \dfrac{15}{60}$ so $R_T = \dfrac{60}{15} = 4 \; \Omega$

7. $\dfrac{1}{R_{parallel}} = \dfrac{1}{R_1} + \dfrac{1}{R_2} = \dfrac{1}{40} + \dfrac{1}{60} = \dfrac{3+2}{120} = \dfrac{5}{120}$ so $R_{parallel} = \dfrac{120}{5} = 24 \; \Omega$

   $R_T = R_{parallel} + R_3 = 24 + 50 = 74 \; \Omega$

Potential divider circuits

1. (a) A potential divider circuit consists of a number of resistors connected in series across a supply.

   (b) to control the voltage across the thermistor

2. (a) $\dfrac{V_1}{V_2} = \dfrac{R_1}{R_2}$

   (b) $V_S = V_1 + V_2$

   $V_1 = V_S \times \dfrac{R_1}{R_1 + R_2}$

3. $V_1 = V_S \times \dfrac{R_1}{R_1 + R_2} = 9.00 \times \dfrac{220}{220 + 180}$

   so $V_1 = 4.95$ V

4. (a)

   Circuit: 2.5 V supply with $R_2 = 1500\,\Omega$ and $R_1 = 1000\,\Omega$ in series; V_1 measured across R_1.

   (b) $V_1 = V_S \times \dfrac{R_1}{R_1 + R_2} = 2.5 \times \dfrac{1000}{1000 + 1500}$

   $= \dfrac{2500}{2500} = 1.0$ V

5. If V_1 is half of V_S then $V_1 = V_2 = \dfrac{V_S}{2}$ so $R_1 = R_2$

   The two resistors have equal values.

Electricity and Energy Answers   23

Electronic systems and circuits

1. (a) an electronic device that converts the electrical energy from the process part of the system into a different form of energy
   (b) an electronic device that converts some form of energy into electrical energy for processing in the next stage of the electronic system

2. (a) light
   (b) sound
   (c) kinetic (rotational)
   (d) kinetic

3. (a) a motor
   (b) a bell or a buzzer
   (c) a loudspeaker
   (d) an LED
   (e) a relay

4. (a) a photovoltaic cell
   (b) a capacitor
   (c) a thermistor
   (d) a microphone
   (e) an LDR

5. (a) a switch or an LDR
   (b) an LDR
   (c) a microphone
   (d) a capacitor
   (e) a thermistor

6. Circuit (i)
   (a) This circuit lights the LED when the temperature of the thermistor rises above a certain value.
   (b) When the temperature of the thermistor rises, its resistance decreases. This causes the voltage at the base of the transistor to rise. When this voltage reaches about 0.7 V, the transistor conducts and the LED emits light.

Circuit (ii)
(a) This circuit lights the LED when the temperature of the thermistor falls below a certain value.

(b) When the temperature of the thermistor falls, its resistance increases. This causes the voltage at the base of the transistor to rise. When this voltage reaches about 0.7 V, the transistor conducts and the LED emits light.

Circuit (iii)
(a) This circuit lights the LED when the intensity of light falling on the LDR rises above a certain value.

(b) When the intensity of light falling on the LDR rises, its resistance decreases. This causes the voltage at the base of the transistor to rise. When this voltage reaches about 0.7 V, the transistor conducts and the LED emits light.

Circuit (iv)
(a) This circuit lights the LED when the intensity of light falling on the LDR falls below a certain value.

(b) When the intensity of light falling on the LDR falls, its resistance increases. This causes the voltage at the base of the transistor to rise. When this voltage reaches about 0.7 V, the transistor conducts and the LED emits light.

Circuits (i) to (iv)
(c) to control the point at which the voltage at the base is sufficient to switch on the transistor; this adjusts the sensitivity of the circuit to temperature or light intensity.

7. When the switch **S** is closed, the capacitor **C** is discharged. This reduces the voltage at the base of the transistor to zero, turning it off. When the switch **S** is opened, the capacitor charges up through the resistor **R** and the voltage across the capacitor **C** rises. When the voltage at the base of the transistor rises to about 0.7 V the transistor switches on and the LED emits light.

Electrical power

Household appliances

1. to change electrical energy from the mains supply into another more useful form of energy, usually heat, light, kinetic or sound

2. (a)

Household appliance	Main energy transformation
toaster	electrical to heat
table lamp	electrical to light
kettle	electrical to heat
vacuum cleaner	electrical to kinetic
electric fire	electrical to heat

   (b) the element; this is made from resistance wire.

3. (a) a measure of the amount of electrical energy it transfers into other forms of energy in a given time

   (b) the watt, W

   (c) the operating voltage and the power rating of the appliance

4. (a)

Household appliance	Approximate power rating (W)
toaster	800 – 1000
hair dryer	500 – 1000
kettle	2000
light bulb	60, 100, 150
electric fire	3000
shaver	10
cooker	12 000

   (b) those which are designed to transform electrical energy into heat energy

5. (a) to connect the appliance to the mains through the plug

   (b) the power rating of the appliance

   (c) The flex can overheat and possibly melt the insulation creating a risk of fire.

6. (a) to protect the flex attached to the appliance from possible damage due to overheating when overloaded

   (b) The fuse is a thin piece of wire which melts when the current drawn by the appliance becomes too great. When this happens the electricity supply to the appliance is cut off, reducing the danger.

7. (a) 3 A and 13 A

   (b) For appliances up to 720 W, use a 3 A fuse; greater than 720 W, use a 13 A fuse.

   (c) Choose the *lowest* value of fuse, either 3 A or 13 A, that is *higher* than the current taken by the appliance.

8. There is a large surge of current when the motor is first switched on. This would melt a 3 A fuse.

Power, energy and time

1. (a) E (b) the joule, J

2. the rate at which energy is transformed from one form into another

3. (a) P
   (b) the watt, W
   (c) 1 watt = 1 joule per second

4. $P = \dfrac{E}{t}$

5. power, $P = 150$ W
   time, $t = 1$ minute $= 60$ s

   $P = \dfrac{E}{t}$ $\therefore 150 = \dfrac{E}{60}$ so $E = 150 \times 60 = 9000$ J, or 9 kJ

6. (a) A kilowatt-hour (kWh) is an alternative unit of energy (often used by power companies).

   (b) To calculate the energy transferred in kilowatt-hours, the formula is the same, $E = Pt$, but use the units of kilowatt and hour for the power and time respectively.

   (c) power, $P = 5.00$ kW
       time, $t = 2$ hours 15 minutes $= 2.25$ hours

       $P = \dfrac{E}{t}$ $\therefore 5.00 = \dfrac{E}{2.25}$ so $E = 5.00 \times 2.25 = 11.3$ kWh

7. 1 kilowatt-hour = 1000 watt-hour = 1000 × 60 × 60 watt-second
   $\hspace{10.5em}$ = 3 600 000 J

8. (a) number of lamps left on = 1000
       power per lamp = 100 W
       total power = 1000 × 100 = 100 000 W = 100 kW
       time left on = 1 hour
       so energy wasted = 100 × 1 = 100 kW h

   (b) cost per kilowatt-hour = 10 p
       so cost of wasted energy = 100 × 10 p = £10.00

   (c) energy wasted by lamps = 100 kW h
       electrical energy needed to produce this wasted energy
       $\hspace{14em}$ = 10 × 100 = 1000 kW h
       This is equivalent to a megawatt of power being wasted every hour.

Power, voltage, current and resistance in electrical circuits

1. (a) $P = V \times I$
   (b) $P = I^2 \times R$
   (c) $P = \dfrac{V^2}{R}$

2. $P = V \times I$ and $V = I \times R$ $P = V \times I$ and $I = \dfrac{V}{R}$

   so $P = (I \times R) \times I$ so $P = V \times \dfrac{V}{R}$

   so $P = I^2 R$ so $P = \dfrac{V^2}{R}$

3. The heating element of an electric fire has a far higher resistance than the flex which connects the fire to the mains. So the rate at which electrical energy is transformed to heat ($I^2 R$) in the heating element is far greater than in the flex even although the current is the same in both.

4. When the current in a lamp is increased, the brightness of the lamp increases because the power developed in it increases.

5. (a)

Appliance	Power (W)	Current (A)
Microwave oven	1380	6.0
Bedside lamp	100	0.43
Sandwich maker	920	4.0
Television	300	1.3

   (b) (i) power, P = 1380 W
   voltage, V = mains voltage = 230 V
   $$\text{current} = \dfrac{\text{power}}{\text{voltage}} = \dfrac{1380}{230} = 6 \text{ A}$$
   This current is greater than 3 A so use a 13 A fuse.

   (ii) power, P = 100 W
   voltage, V = mains voltage = 230 V
   $$\text{current} = \dfrac{\text{power}}{\text{voltage}} = \dfrac{100}{230} = 0.43 \text{ A}$$
   This current is less than 3 A so a 3 A fuse should be fitted.

6. current, I = 3.0 A
   voltage, V = 12 V
   $P = V \times I = 12 \times 3.0 = 36$ W

Electricity and Energy Answers

7. voltage, V = mains voltage = 230 V
   power, P = 690 W
   $P = V \times I$ ∴ $690 = 230 \times I$
   so $I = \dfrac{690}{230} = 3$ A

8. resistance, $R = 10\,\text{k}\Omega = 10 \times 10^3\,\Omega$
   current, $I = 5.0\,\text{mA} = 5.0 \times 10^{-3}$ A
   power (rate of energy transformation), $P = I^2 R$
   so $P = (5.0 \times 10^{-3})^2 \times 10 \times 10^3 = 0.25$ W, or 0.25 J every second

9. power, P = 60 W
   current, I = 0.25 A
   $P = I^2 R$ ∴ $60 = 0.25^2 \times R$
   so $R = \dfrac{60}{0.25^2} = 960\,\Omega$

10. input voltage = $10\,\text{mV} = 10 \times 10^{-3}$ V
    input resistance = $10\,\text{k}\Omega = 10 \times 10^3\,\Omega$
    input power, $P_{in} = \dfrac{V^2}{R} = \dfrac{(10 \times 10^{-3})^2}{10 \times 10^3} = 1 \times 10^{-8}$ W

11. current, I = 0.25 A
    voltage, V = 3.0 V
    $P = V \times I = 3.0 \times 0.25 = 0.75$ W

12. power, P = 5.0 W
    voltage, V = 12 V
    $P = \dfrac{V^2}{R}$ ∴ $5.0 = \dfrac{12^2}{R}$ so $R = \dfrac{144}{5.0} = 29\,\Omega$

13. (a) resistance, R = 92 Ω
       voltage, V = 230 V
       $I = \dfrac{V}{R} = \dfrac{230}{92} = 2.5$ A
    (b) The current is less than 3 A, so use a 3 A fuse.

Specific heat capacity

Temperature and heat energy

1. (a) an instrument used to measure temperature

    (b) Thermometers are able to measure temperatures because they make use of some physical property that changes with temperature, and which can be measured.

2.

(a) *Type of thermometer*	(b) *Physical property that changes with temperature*
Liquid in glass (mercury or alcohol)	Volume of liquid increases as temperature increases
Thermocouple	Voltage generated increases as temperature increases
Liquid crystal	Crystals change colour as temperature changes
Bimetallic strip (rotary thermometer or Rototherm)	Metals expand at different rates when the temperature increases
Digital thermometer with semiconductor probe sensor	Resistance of semiconductor probe changes as the temperature changes

3. liquid   scale   thin tube   glass case

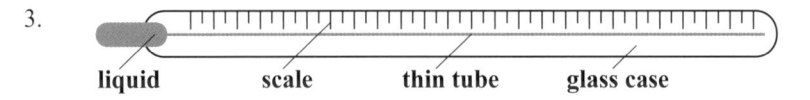

    The liquid, usually mercury or alcohol, expands when the temperature increases. The length of the liquid column in the thin tube gives an indication of the temperature and this is read on the scale.

4. a measure of how hot or cold the object is

5. Celsius or centigrade scale; kelvin scale

6. As the temperature of a gas increases, the mean (average) kinetic energy of its particles **increases** and they move **faster**.

7. (a) **Temperature** is a measure of how hot or cold an object is. It is usually measured in **degrees Celsius**.

    (b) Heat is a form of **energy** and is measured in **joules**.

    (c) Putting **heat** energy into an object usually makes its **temperature** increase.

8. Heat travels from a region of **higher** temperature to a region of **lower** temperature.

9. temperature difference between the hot region and the cold region, e.g. the inside and the outside of a house

Calculations

1. (a) The amount of heat energy is different.
    (b) The amount of heat energy depends on the **specific heat capacity** which is different for different substances.

2. (a) It takes twice as much energy.
    (b) The amount of heat energy depends on the **mass** of the substance.

3. (a) It takes half as much energy.
    (b) The amount of heat energy depends on the **rise in temperature**.

4. (a) It takes the same amount of energy.
    (b) The mass, rise in temperature and specific heat capacity are the same.

5. the amount of energy in joules needed to change the temperature of 1 kg of the substance by 1 °C

6. (a) $E_h = cm\Delta T$ (b) E_h is heat measured in joules, J
    c is specific heat capacity measured in joules per kilogram per degree Celsius, J kg^{-1} $°C^{-1}$
    m is mass measured in kilograms, kg
    ΔT is change in temperature measured in degrees Celsius, °C

7. specific heat capacity, $c = 902$ J kg^{-1} $°C^{-1}$
    mass, $m = 1.00$ kg
    change in temperature, $\Delta T = 10.0$ °C
    $E_h = cm\Delta T = 902 \times 1.00 \times 10.0 = 9020$ J

8. specific heat capacity, $c = 4180$ J kg^{-1} $°C^{-1}$
    mass, $m = 2.00$ kg
    change in temperature, $\Delta T = (90.0 - 20.0) = 70.0$ °C
    $E_h = cm\Delta T = 4180 \times 2.00 \times 70.0 = 585\ 200$ J
    (585 000 J, or 585 kJ to 3 significant figures)

9. A lot of heat is transferred to the surroundings, e.g. can, air.

10. specific heat capacity, $c = 2400$ J kg^{-1} $°C^{-1}$
    mass, $m = 5.0$ kg
    energy, $E_h = 720\ 000$ J
    $E_h = cm\Delta T \quad \therefore 720\ 000 = 2400 \times 5.0 \times \Delta T \quad$ so $\Delta T = \dfrac{720\ 000}{2400 \times 5.0} = 60\ °C$

Electricity and Energy Answers

11. power rating, $P = 2.2$ kW $= 2200$ W
    mass of water, $m = 1.5$ kg
    change in temperature, $\Delta T = (100 - 20) = 80\ °C$
    specific heat capacity, $c = 4180$ J kg^{-1} °C^{-1}
    $P \times t = cm\Delta T$ ∴ $2200 \times t = 4180 \times 1.5 \times 80$

    so $t = \dfrac{4180 \times 1.5 \times 80}{2200} = 228$ s, or 3 minutes 48 s

12. (a) Although energy can be transformed from one type to another, it can neither be created nor destroyed.

    (b) mass of car, $m = 1000$ kg
    speed of car, $v = 4.0$ m s^{-1}
    mass of brake lining material $= 0.5$ kg
    specific heat capacity of brake lining material $= 500$ J kg^{-1} °C^{-1}
    kinetic energy of car: $E_k = \tfrac{1}{2}mv^2 = \tfrac{1}{2} \times 1000 \times 4.0^2 = 8000$ J
    All of this energy is converted into heat, so:

    $E_h = cm\Delta T$ ∴ $8000 = 500 \times 0.5 \times \Delta T$ so $\Delta T = \dfrac{8000}{500 \times 0.5} = 32\ °C$

Gas laws and the kinetic model

Pressure

1. force per unit area exerted on a surface

2. (a) p (b)   pascal, Pa

3. newtons per square metre, N m^{-2}

4. (a) $p = \dfrac{F}{A}$

    (b) p is pressure measured in pascals, Pa
         F is force measured in newtons, N
         A is area measured in square metres, m^2

5. weight (force), $F = 5900$ N
    area, $A = 0.08$ m^2
$$p = \frac{F}{A} = \frac{5900}{0.08} = 73\,750 \text{ Pa} \quad \left(74\,000 \text{ Pa, or } 74 \text{ kPa, to 2 significant figures}\right)$$

6. weight (force), $F = 500$ N
    area, $A = 1 \text{ cm}^2 = 1 \times 10^{-4}$ m^2
$$p = \frac{F}{A} = \frac{500}{1 \times 10^{-4}} = 5 \times 10^6 \text{ Pa, or } 5000 \text{ kPa}$$

7. The same force (weight) is spread over a larger area so the pressure is less.

8. The edge of the sharp knife is narrower (smaller surface area).
    The same force results in a greater pressure and makes cutting easier.

The kinetic model

1. (a) Pollen grains or smoke particles viewed under a microscope are seen to be in constant random motion.

    (b) The random motion is caused by collisions with air particles which are too small to be seen but which are moving in all directions.

2. (a) The kinetic model of matter describes how **solids**, **liquids** and **gases** behave by considering how the **particles** that make up matter are arranged and move.

    (b) In a **solid**, the **particles** are closely packed, **vibrating slowly** about fixed positions in ordered rows.

    (c) In a **liquid**, the **particles** are also **close together** but are **free to move** anywhere in the material.

    (d) In a **gas**, the **particles** are **very far apart** and move **very fast** in all directions.

    (e) The **particles** of a **gas** completely fill all the space of the container.

3. (a) Many millions of particles, spaced far apart, moving in random directions at different speeds.

    (b) The volume of the gas is the volume of the container; the volume of the particles is negligible.

    (c) Particles only affect each other when they collide.

    (d) As the temperature increases the speed and the average kinetic energy of the particles increases.

4. (a) The particles exert a force.

    (b) Pressure is the force of all the particles divided by the area of the walls.

    (c) particles moving faster (higher temperature) or greater number of collisions (decreasing volume)

The gas laws: volume and pressure

1. pV = constant

2. The pressure of a gas inside a closed syringe is changed by pressing the plunger and each new volume of gas and pressure is recorded. To keep the gas at a constant temperature the plunger is pressed slowly.

   or

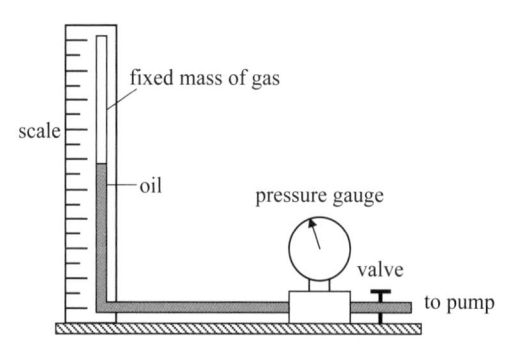

   [Diagram: apparatus showing a vertical tube with scale, fixed mass of gas at top, oil below, connected horizontally to a pressure gauge and valve leading to pump]

   Use the apparatus shown. Vary the pressure of the fixed mass of gas trapped in the tube by using the pump. Read the pressure of the gas on the pressure gauge. Read the length of the gas column on the scale. (The volume of gas varies as the length of the column.) Repeat for different pressures. Plot a graph of pressure against volume and a graph of pressure against 1/volume.
   This experiment shows that the pressure of a fixed mass of gas varies inversely as its volume.

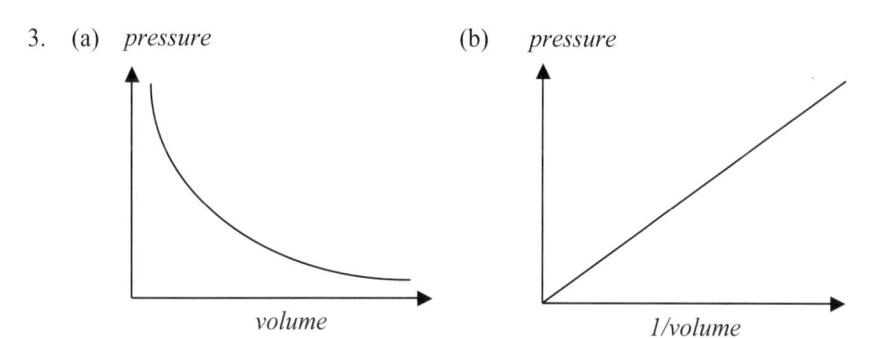

3. (a) *pressure* vs *volume* — curve decreasing (inverse relationship)

   (b) *pressure* vs *1/volume* — straight line through origin

4. The pressure of a fixed mass of gas varies inversely with the volume, as long as the temperature of the gas stays the same.

Electricity and Energy Answers

5. (a) $p_1V_1 = p_2V_2$

   (b) consistent units on both sides of the equation

6. $V_1 = 2$ litres
$p_1 = 5 \times 10^5$ Pa
$p_2 = 1 \times 10^5$ Pa
$p_1V_1 = p_2V_2 \quad \therefore 5 \times 10^5 \times 2 = 1 \times 10^5 \times V_2 \quad$ so $V_2 = \dfrac{5 \times 10^5 \times 2}{1 \times 10^5} = 10$ litres

7. $V_1 = 1$ litre $= 1000$ ml
$V_2 = 1000$ ml $+ 10$ ml $= 1010$ ml
$p_1 = 1.0 \times 10^5$ Pa
$p_1V_1 = p_2V_2 \quad \therefore 1.0 \times 10^5 \times 1000 = p_2 \times 1010$

so $p_2 = \dfrac{1.00 \times 10^5 \times 1000}{1010} = 0.99 \times 10^5$ Pa, or 99 kPa

8. Because temperature is constant, average kinetic energy and speed of the particles stays the same. Increasing volume increases the distance particles travel between collisions so there are fewer collisions per second. This means pressure is lower.

Different temperature scales

1. (a) −273 °C   (b) 0 K   (c) kelvin, K

2. (a) −273 °C or 0 K

   (b) This is the temperature at which the particles have lost all their kinetic energy. They are not moving.

3. (a) kelvin = degrees Celsius + 273

   (b) degree Celsius = kelvin − 273

4. (a) (i) 0 K   (ii) 300 K   (iii) 373 K
   (b) (i) −273 °C   (ii) 0 °C   (iii) 127 °C

5. They are both the same.

6. 50 K

Electricity and Energy Answers

The gas laws: pressure and temperature

1. (a) $\dfrac{p}{T}$ = constant (b) absolute scale of temperature

2. Use the apparatus shown. Increase the temperature of the fixed mass of gas in the flask by using the heat source. Read the temperature of the gas on the thermometer. Read the pressure of the gas on the pressure gauge. Record the temperature and the pressure of the gas at various different temperatures. Plot graphs of pressure against temperature in °C and in kelvin.
This experiment shows that the pressure of a fixed mass of gas increases as its temperature increases but does not show the exact relationship when temperature is measured in degrees Celsius. A graph of pressure against temperature in kelvin shows that pressure varies directly as temperature in kelvin.

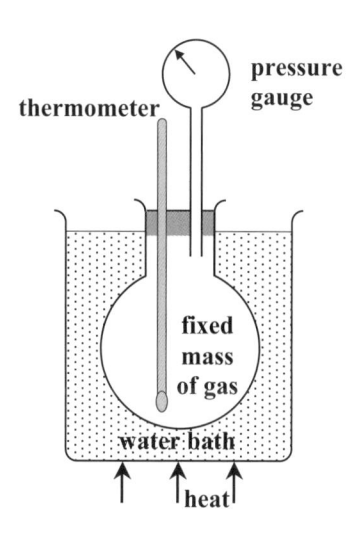

3. (a) graph of pressure vs temperature (°C), intercept at −273, dashed extrapolation to 100
   (b) graph of pressure vs temperature (K), straight line through origin

4. The pressure of a fixed mass of gas at constant volume is directly proportional to the absolute temperature.

5. (a) $\dfrac{p_1}{T_1} = \dfrac{p_2}{T_2}$

   (b) consistent pressure units; temperature in kelvin

Electricity and Energy Answers 39

6. $p_1 = 2.0 \times 10^5$ Pa
   $T_1 = 27\,°C = 300$ K
   $T_2 = 57\,°C = 330$ K

   $\dfrac{p_1}{T_1} = \dfrac{p_2}{T_2} \quad \therefore \dfrac{2.0 \times 10^5}{300} = \dfrac{p_2}{330} \quad \text{so } p_2 = \dfrac{2.0 \times 10^5 \times 330}{300}$

   $= 2.2 \times 10^5$ Pa, or 220 kPa

7. $p_1 = 1$ At $= 1.0 \times 10^5$ Pa
   $T_1 = $ T K
   $T_2 = $ 2T K

   $\dfrac{p_1}{T_1} = \dfrac{p_2}{T_2} \quad \therefore \dfrac{1.0 \times 10^5}{T} = \dfrac{p_2}{2T} \quad \text{so } p_2 = \dfrac{1.0 \times 10^5 \times 2T}{T} = 2.0 \times 10^5$ Pa, or 200 kPa

8. Because the volume does not change, the particles travel the same distance between collisions. Since the temperature increases, the average kinetic energy and speed of the particles increase. This means there are more collisions in the same time and so the pressure increases.

The gas laws: volume and temperature

1. (a) $\dfrac{V}{T}$ = constant (b) absolute scale of temperature

2. Use the apparatus shown. Increase the temperature of the fixed mass of gas trapped under the seal in the capillary tube by using the heat source. Read the length of the gas column on the scale. (The volume of gas varies as the length of the column.) Read the temperature of the gas on the thermometer. Record the volume and the temperature of the gas at various different temperatures. Plot graphs of volume against temperature in °C and in kelvin.
This experiment shows that the volume of a fixed mass of gas varies directly as its temperature in kelvin.

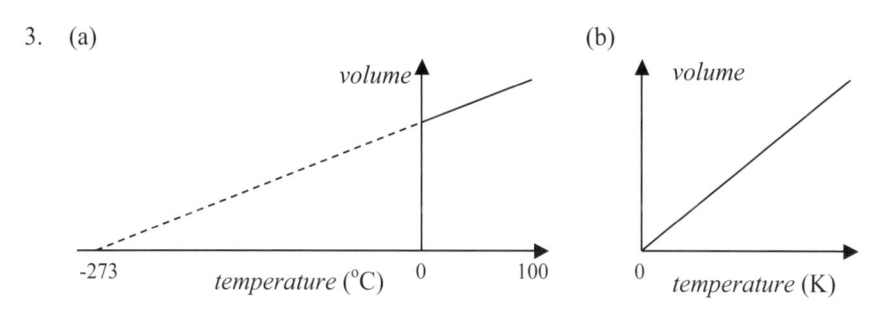

3. (a)   (b)

4. The volume of a fixed mass of gas at constant pressure is directly proportional to the absolute temperature.

5. (a) $\dfrac{V_1}{T_1} = \dfrac{V_2}{T_2}$

   (b) consistant volume units; temperature in kelvins

Electricity and Energy Answers   41

6. $T_1 = 27\ °C = 300\ K$
   $V_1 = 0.10\ m^3$
   $T_2 = 177\ °C = 450\ K$

   $\dfrac{V_1}{T_1} = \dfrac{V_2}{T_2}\quad \therefore \dfrac{0.10}{300} = \dfrac{V_2}{450}\quad \text{so } V_2 = \dfrac{0.10 \times 450}{300} = 0.15\ m^3$

7. $T_1 = -3\ °C = 270\ K$
   $V_1 = 0.9V$
   $V_2 = V$

   $\dfrac{V_1}{T_1} = \dfrac{V_2}{T_2}\quad \therefore \dfrac{0.9V}{270} = \dfrac{V}{T_2}\quad \text{so } T_2 = \dfrac{V \times 270}{0.9V} = 300\ K$

   Temperature in degrees Celsius = 300 – 273 = 27 °C

8. Because the temperature increases, the average kinetic energy and speed of the particles increase. If the volume did not increase the pressure would increase because there would be more collisions per second. So the volume increases to keep the number of collisions per second, and therefore the pressure, the same.

The gas laws: the combined gas equation

1. $\dfrac{pV}{T} = \text{constant}$

2. $\dfrac{p_1 V_1}{T_1} = \dfrac{p_2 V_2}{T_2}$

3. $V_1 = 6.0\,\text{m}^3$
   $p_1 = 1.0 \times 10^5\,\text{Pa}$
   $T_1 = 27\,°\text{C} = 300\,\text{K}$
   $p_2 = 5.5 \times 10^5\,\text{Pa}$
   $T_2 = -23\,°\text{C} = 250\,\text{K}$

   $\dfrac{p_1 V_1}{T_1} = \dfrac{p_2 V_2}{T_2}$

   $\therefore \dfrac{1.0 \times 10^5 \times 6.0}{300} = \dfrac{5.5 \times 10^5 \times V_2}{250}$

   so $V_2 = \dfrac{1.0 \times 10^5 \times 6.0 \times 250}{5.5 \times 10^5 \times 300} = 0.91\,\text{m}^3$

Unit 2   Waves and Radiation

Wave parameters and behaviours

Waves and energy

1. A wave is a regular disturbance that carries energy and has no mass.

2. Waves transfer **energy** from one place to another; they are created by **vibrations**.

3. e.g. water waves; radio and television waves; light waves

Wave parameters

1. (a) With a transverse wave, the particles of the medium vibrate at right angles to the direction in which the energy is carried. With a longitudinal wave the particles that carry the energy are alternately pushed together and separated apart, in the direction that the energy is transferred.
   (b) water waves; television and radio waves; light waves
   (c) sound waves

2. (a) the number of waves that are made in a given time period
   (b) f
   (c) the hertz, Hz
   (d) One hertz is one wave per second.

3. (a) the time it takes to make one complete wave
   (b) T
   (c) the second, s

4. (a) the distance from any point on one wave to the corresponding point on the next wave along, e.g. from the top of one crest to the top of the next crest
   (b) λ
   (c) Since wavelength is a distance, it is measured in metres, m.

5. (a) the distance the wave covers in a given time period
   (b) v
   (c) the metre per second, m s^{-1}

6. (a) the height of the wave from the centre position to the top of a crest **or** from the centre position to the bottom of a trough
   (b) a
   (c) the metre, m

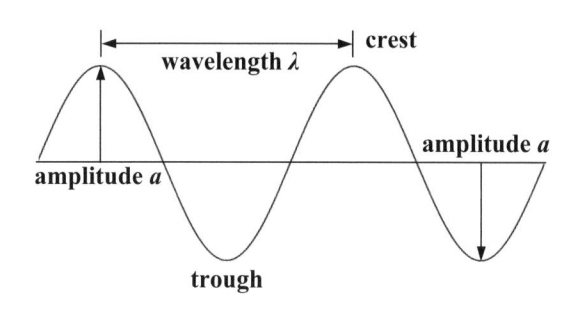

7.

```
       |◄──────────►| crest
        wavelength λ
         ╱╲          ╱╲
        ╱  ╲        ╱  ╲         amplitude a
       ╱    ╲      ╱    ╲         ↓
  ────╱──────╲────╱──────╲────────
     amplitude a  ╲      ╱
                   ╲    ╱
                    ╲  ╱
                     ╲╱
                   trough
```

Calculations

1. no. of vibrations = 81 600
   time, t = 4 minutes = 240 s

   $$f = \frac{\text{no. of vibrations}}{\text{time in seconds}}$$

   $$= \frac{81\ 600}{240}$$

   $$= 340\ \text{Hz}$$

2. $T = \dfrac{1}{f}$

3. wave frequency, $f = 0.21$ Hz
   $T = \dfrac{1}{f} \quad \therefore T = \dfrac{1}{0.21} = 4.8\ \text{s}$

4. (a) $v = \dfrac{d}{t}$ (b) v is speed measured in metres per second, m s^{-1}
   d is distance measured in metres, m
   t is time measured in seconds, s

5. speed of sound, $v = 340$ m s^{-1}
   time, $t = 5.0$ s
   $v = \dfrac{d}{t} \quad \therefore 340 = \dfrac{d}{5.0}$ so $d = 340 \times 5.0 = 1700$ m, or 1.7 km

6. distance, $d = 1.7$ m
   time, $t = 5.0 \times 10^{-3}$ s
   $v = \dfrac{d}{t} = \dfrac{1.7}{5.0 \times 10^{-3}} = 340\ \text{m s}^{-1}$

7. time, $t = 3.00$ s
   speed, $v = 340$ m s^{-1}
   $v = \dfrac{d}{t} \quad \therefore 340 = \dfrac{d}{3.00}$ so $d = 340 \times 3.00 = 1020$ m

8. speed of sound, $v = 340$ m s^{-1}
   distance, $d = 1.36$ km $= 1360$ m
   $v = \dfrac{d}{t} \quad \therefore 340 = \dfrac{1360}{t}$ so $t = \dfrac{1360}{340} = 4\ \text{s}$

9. time, $t = 0.2$ ms $= 0.0002$ s
   distance, $d = 0.3$ m
   $$v = \frac{d}{t} = \frac{0.3}{0.0002} = 1500 \text{ m s}^{-1}$$

10. time, $t = 0.50$ s
    distance, $d = 2.6$ km $= 2600$ m
    $$v = \frac{d}{t} = \frac{2600}{0.50} = 5200 \text{ m s}^{-1}$$

11. distance, $d = 8.8$ m
    time, $t = 4.0$ s
    $$v = \frac{d}{t} = \frac{8.8}{4.0} = 2.2 \text{ m s}^{-1}$$

12. time, $t = 5.0$ s
    speed, $v = 3.0$ m s^{-1}
    $$v = \frac{d}{t} \quad \therefore 3.0 = \frac{d}{5.0} \quad \text{so } d = 3.0 \times 5.0 = 15 \text{ m}$$

13. distance, $d = 14$ m
    speed of waves, $v = 4.0$ m s^{-1}
    $$v = \frac{d}{t} \quad \therefore 4.0 = \frac{14}{t} \quad \text{so } t = \frac{14}{4.0} = 3.5 \text{ s}$$

14. (a) $v = f\lambda$ (b) v is speed measured in metres per second, m s^{-1}
    f is frequency measured in hertz, Hz
    λ is wavelength measured in metres, m

15. frequency, $f = 10$ Hz
    wavelength, $\lambda = 0.4$ m
    $$v = f\lambda = 10 \times 0.4 = 4 \text{ m s}^{-1}$$

16. frequency, $f = 262$ Hz
    speed of waves, $v = 340$ m s^{-1}
    $$v = f\lambda \quad \therefore 340 = 262 \times \lambda \quad \text{so } \lambda = \frac{340}{262} = 1.3 \text{ m}$$

17. wavelength, $\lambda = 0.50$ m
    speed of waves, $v = 0.25$ m s^{-1}
    $$v = f\lambda \quad \therefore 0.25 = f \times 0.50 \quad \text{so } f = \frac{0.25}{0.50} = 0.5 \text{ Hz}$$

18. wavelength, $\lambda = 2.8\,\text{cm} = 2.8\times 10^{-2}\,\text{m}$
    speed of waves, $v = 3\times 10^8\,\text{m s}^{-1}$

    $v = f\lambda \quad \therefore 3\times 10^8 = f\times 2.8\times 10^{-2} \quad \text{so } f = \dfrac{3\times 10^8}{2.8\times 10^{-2}} = 1.1\times 10^{10}\,\text{Hz}$

19. In a time equal to one period of the wave, a wave travels a distance of one wavelength, so if $t = T$, then $d = \lambda$.

    $T = \dfrac{1}{f} \quad \text{so } f = \dfrac{1}{T}$

    $\therefore f\lambda = \dfrac{\lambda}{T} = \dfrac{d}{t}$

Diffraction

1. an effect which causes waves to bend as they go past the end of a barrier or through a gap

2. Long wavelength waves diffract more than short wavelength waves.

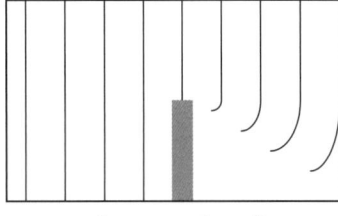

long wavelength 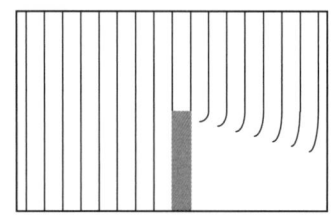   **short wavelength**

3. Radio waves have longer wavelengths than television waves. In areas where there is an obstacle such as a hill between the transmitting aerial and the receiver, radio reception will be better than television reception. This is because longer wavelength radio waves diffract more than shorter wavelength television waves.

4. Long waves in the low frequency band diffract more and they also reflect off the ionosphere during the night.

5. (a) Semi-circular waves are formed on the other side of the gap.   (b) Straight waves, diffracted at the edges, are formed.

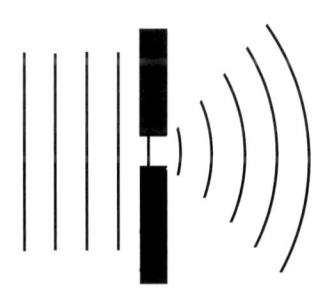

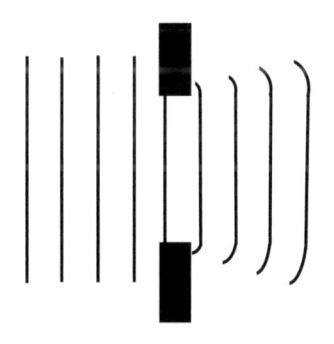

Electromagnetic spectrum

The bands of the electromagnetic spectrum

1. (a) gamma rays, X-rays, ultraviolet, visible light, infrared, microwaves, TV and radio

   (b) They all travel at the speed of light (3×10^8 m s^{-1} in a vacuum).

   (c) the wavelengths and frequencies

2. (a)   (b)   (c)

Type of radiation	Approx wavelength range (m)	Approx frequency range (Hz)	Source	Detector
gamma rays	$10^{-13} - 10^{-10}$	$10^{21} - 10^{18}$	decay of atomic nuclei	geiger counter
X-rays	$10^{-12} - 10^{-8}$	$10^{20} - 10^{16}$	high voltage vacuum tube	photographic film
ultraviolet	$10^{-9} - 10^{-7}$	$10^{17} - 10^{15}$	Sun; 'black light' lamps	fluorescent material
visible light	$10^{-7} - 10^{-6}$	$10^{15} - 10^{14}$	Sun; stars; electric lamp	eye and photographic film
infrared	$10^{-6} - 10^{-3}$	$10^{14} - 10^{11}$	Sun; hot bodies	thermometer
microwaves	$10^{-4} - 10$	$10^{12} - 10^{7}$	vacuum tubes; field-effect transistor	diode probe
TV & radio	$10^{-1} - 10^{4}$	$10^{9} - 10^{4}$	stars; aerials	aerial and TV or radio

3. the higher the frequency, the greater the energy

4. (a) visible light

   (b) gamma rays; X-rays; ultraviolet; infrared

Applications of the electromagnetic spectrum

1. (a) a narrow, intense high energy beam of light of only one frequency
   (b) from the initial letters of **L**ight **A**mplification by **S**timulated **E**mission of **R**adiation
   (c) reading barcodes on goods; in CD and DVD players; in industry as precise cutting and welding tools; disco and club lighting; for communication along optical fibres; in medicine, e.g. for treating tumours and for eye surgery

2. speed, $v = 3 \times 10^8$ ms^{-1}
   wavelength, $\lambda = 660$ nm $= 660 \times 10^{-9}$ m
   $v = f\lambda \quad \therefore 3 \times 10^8 = f \times 660 \times 10^{-9} \quad$ so $f = \dfrac{3 \times 10^8}{660 \times 10^{-9}} = 4.55 \times 10^{14}$ Hz

3. (a) heat
   (b) our skin
   (c) e.g.
       medical - breast cancer detection; detection and treatment of soft tissue (muscle) injury; blood flow in veins
       police – suspect pursuit and capture; surveillance and stakeout; riot control
       fire and safety – victim location; search and rescue; navigation
       marine – search and rescue; oil spill location; aid to navigation
       environmental – wildlife observation and control; weather forecasting; predicting volcano activity
       transport – traffic reports in fog and poor visibility; increased 'visibility' in poor conditions; engine maintenance and fault diagnosis
       industry – non-destructive testing; evaluation of heat loss from buildings

4. (a) Small quantities of ultraviolet radiation help to produce the essential chemical, vitamin D. Treatment with ultraviolet radiation helps to reduce vitamin D deficiency.
   (b) (i) e.g. to treat skin conditions such as acne; to sterilise medical equipment
       (ii) e.g. for hand stamping at admission gates; for security marking of products, e.g. bank notes
   (c) Suntan creams 'block' the ultraviolet radiation from getting to the skin.
   (d) The ozone layer acts as a filter that stops too much ultraviolet radiation reaching us from space. A result of the thinning of the ozone layer is that there are more cases of skin cancer.

5. (a) X-rays are high-energy rays that pass through most materials to some extent.
   (b) X-rays darken photographic film; they cause fluorescence from special screens.

6. (a) X-rays pass through soft tissue such as skin and muscle.
   (b) X-rays are absorbed by dense tissue such as bone.

7. to obtain images of the contents of luggage

8. (a) Since X-rays are high-energy rays, they are harmful to cells.
   (b) wear lead gloves or lead-lined aprons; operate machine remotely from behind a screen.
   (c) reproductive cells

9. Gamma rays are emitted (given out) by radioactive materials.

10. (a) Any bacteria on the instruments are killed by the exposure to the radiation. Since the instruments are not made of living tissue, they are unaffected. The instruments do not become radioactive since no radioactive material touches the instrument.
    (b) e.g. killing cancer cells

11. (a) waves
    (b) energy
    (c) 3×10^8 m s^{-1}

12. time, $t = 1.2$ s
    speed, $v = 3.0 \times 10^8$ m s^{-1}
    $v = \dfrac{d}{t}$ $\therefore 3.0 \times 10^8 = \dfrac{d}{1.2}$ so $d = 3.0 \times 10^8 \times 1.2 = 3.6 \times 10^8$ m

13. frequency, $f = 909$ kHz $= 909 \times 10^3$ Hz
    speed, $v = 3.0 \times 10^8$ m s^{-1}
    $v = f\lambda$ $\therefore 3.0 \times 10^8 = 909 \times 10^3 \times \lambda$ so $\lambda = \dfrac{3.0 \times 10^8}{909 \times 10^3} = 330$ m

14. wavelength, $\lambda = 194$ m
    speed, $v = 3.0 \times 10^8$ m s^{-1}

    $v = f\lambda \quad \therefore 3.0 \times 10^8 = f \times 194 \quad \text{so } f = \dfrac{3.0 \times 10^8}{194} = 1.546 \times 10^6$ Hz, or 1546 Hz

15. They travel in straight lines and do not follow the curvature of the Earth.

16. (a) e.g. satellite communication; mobile phones; cooking
    (b) They pass through the ionosphere.

Light

1. (a) Refraction is the change in speed of light. This happens when light goes from one substance (or medium) into another, e.g. from air into glass. When a ray of light is refracted, its direction usually changes.

    (b) e.g. telescope; microscope; camera; binoculars; data projector

2. (a) the angle between the incident ray and the normal

    (b) the angle between the refracted ray and the normal

    (c) a line drawn at right angles (perpendicular) to the glass surface at the point where the ray meets the glass

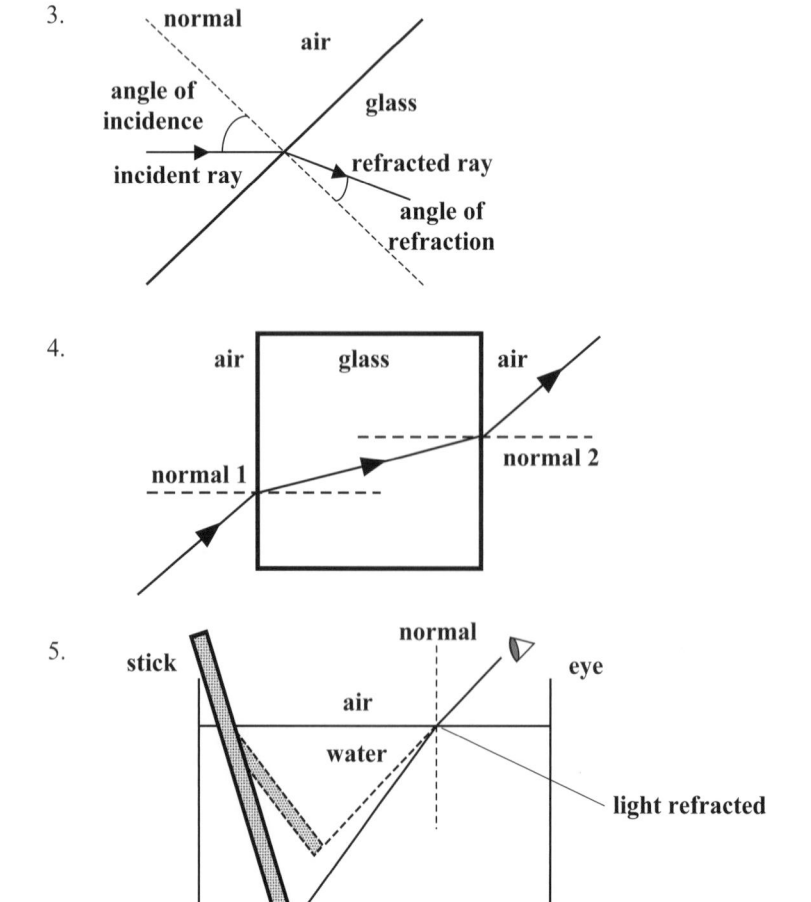

3.

4.

5.

6. The wave speed decreases.

7. (a) When a wave refracts, the wave speed **always** changes.
   (b) When a wave refracts, the frequency **never** changes.
   (c) When a wave refracts, the wavelength **always** changes.
   (d) When a wave refracts, the direction **sometimes** changes.

8. (a) A converging lens is thicker in the centre than at the edges.

   (b) A diverging lens is thinner in the centre than at the edges.

9. (a)

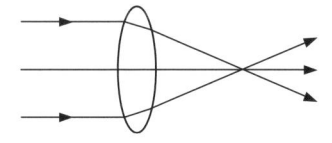

   (b)

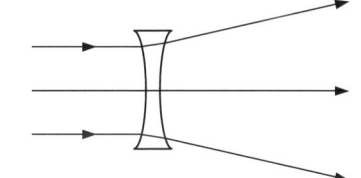

10. (a)

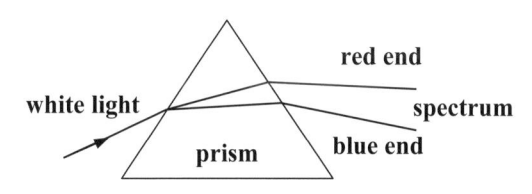

    white light → prism → spectrum (red end, blue end)

    (b) White light is made up of different colours of light, each of which has a different wavelength. A prism separates the white light into the spectrum of colours because different wavelengths are refracted by different amounts at each of the two boundaries.

Nuclear radiation

The nature of radiation

1. An atom consists of a nucleus containing protons and neutrons, surrounded by orbiting electrons.

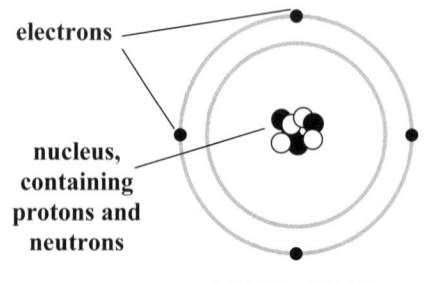

    electrons

    nucleus, containing protons and neutrons

    NOT TO SCALE

2. (a) protons, neutrons and electrons

    (b) protons and neutrons approximately equal in mass; electrons about $\frac{1}{2000}$ that of a proton and neutron

    (c) the nucleus

3. (a) proton - positive

    (b) electron - negative

    (c) neutron - no charge

4. (a) Atoms of the same element that have different numbers of neutrons in the nucleus.

    (b) radioisotopes (radionuclides)

    (c) The nuclei of the atoms break up (decay) with the emission of radiation.

5. The energy may be absorbed.

6. alpha (α),   beta (β),   gamma (γ)

7. Alpha radiation consists of positively charged particles. An alpha particle is a helium nucleus. It is made up of two protons and two neutrons, so it has a mass number of 4 and a charge of +2.

8. Beta radiation consists of high energy electrons. A beta particle has neglible mass and a charge of –1.

9. (a) Gamma radiation is a burst of electromagnetic radiation of very short wavelength and high energy.

   (b) When an atom decays by emitting either alpha or beta particles, the nucleus that remains is often unstable. It can become more stable by rearranging itself and in the process it emits a burst of gamma radiation.

10. (a) Alpha radiation can only travel a few centimetres in air.
    Beta radiation can travel through a few metres of air.
    Air does not absorb gamma radiation.

    (b) Alpha radiation is absorbed by thin paper.
    A few millimetres of aluminium will absorb beta radiation.
    Gamma radiation is absorbed by a minimum of a few centimetres of lead.

11. gamma radiation

12. An atom contains equal numbers of protons and electrons, and therefore equal numbers of positive and negative charges.

13. (a) When an atom is ionised it gains electrons to become negatively charged or loses electrons to become positively charged. The charged atom is known as an ion.

    (b) alpha radiation

Dosimetry

1. (a) The rate at which a radioactive source decays is called the activity of the source. It is the number of nuclei which disintegrate in a given time period.

    (b) A

    (c) the becquerel, Bq

    (d) One becquerel is one nucleus decaying per second.

    (e) $A = \dfrac{N}{t}$

2. The activity depends on the mass.

3. The mass of radium in 1 g of radium oxide will be less than that in 1 g of radium.

4. activity, $A = 21.0$ Bq $= 21$ nuclei decaying per second
    time, $t = 1$ hour $= 3600$ seconds

    $A = \dfrac{N}{t}$ so $21.0 = \dfrac{N}{3600}$

    $\therefore N = 21.0 \times 3600 = 75\,600$

5. time, $t = 20$ s
    number of disintegrations, $N = 8 \times 10^7$

    $A = \dfrac{N}{t}$ $\therefore A = \dfrac{8 \times 10^7}{20} = 4 \times 10^6 = 4$ MBq

6. (a) When a radioactive source decays, it gives out energy. This energy can be absorbed by another material and can cause damage to the material. The absorbed dose is the energy absorbed per unit mass of the absorbing material.

    (b) D

    (c) the gray, Gy

    (d) One gray is one joule per kilogram (J kg^{-1}).

    (e) $D = \dfrac{E}{m}$

7. The effect is related to the absorbed dose, D.
    Since the infant has a smaller mass than the adult, the radiation has a greater effect.

8. mass, $m = 50$ g $= 50 \times 10^{-3}$ kg
absorbed dose, $D = 20$ Gy

$D = \dfrac{E}{m}$ $\therefore 20 = \dfrac{E}{50 \times 10^{-3}}$ so $E = 20 \times 50 \times 10^{-3} = 1$ J

9. (a) Different types of radiation have different effects on living cells. The radiation weighting factor allows the ability of different types of radiation to damage living cells to be compared.

   (b) w_r

   (c) The radiation weighting factor for radiation does not have a unit because it is not a physical quantity. It is a number that gives the relative harm done to cells by different types of radiation.

10.

Type of radiation	Radiation weighting factor
alpha particles (α)	20
beta particles (β)	1
gamma rays (γ)	1
slow (thermal) neutrons	3

11. (a) Radiation damage in biological systems depends on the type of radiation as well as how the energy that it releases is distributed. The equivalent dose is a measure of the biological effect of radiation.

    (b) H

    (c) the sievert, Sv

    (d) $H = Dw_r$

12. (a) the type of tissue that absorbs the radiation; the nature of the radiation that is absorbed; the energy of the radiation that is absorbed; the mass of absorbing material; the distance from the source

    (b) shield from the source; limit the time of exposure; increase the distance from the source

13. (a) The equivalent dose rate is a measure of the rate of the biological effect of radiation.

    (b) $\dot{H}$

    (c) any of sievert/millisievert/microsievert per second/minute/hour

    (d) $\dot{H} = \dfrac{H}{t}$

14. absorbed dose, $D = 40\ \mu Gy = 40 \times 10^{-6}$ Gy
    time, $t = 8$ hours
    radiation weighting factor, $w_r = 20$ (alpha particles)

    (a) $H = Dw_r$ $\therefore H = 40 \times 10^{-6} \times 20 = 800\ \mu Sv$

    (b) $\dot{H} = \dfrac{H}{t} = \dfrac{800}{8} = 100\ \mu Sv\,h^{-1}$

15. slow neutrons: absorbed dose, $D = 200\ \mu Gy$;
                     radiation weighting factor, $w_r = 3$
    gamma radiation: absorbed dose, $D = 50\ \mu Gy$;
                     radiation weighting factor, $w_r = 1$

    (a) $H = Dw_r$ (slow neutrons) $+ Dw_r$ (gamma radiation)
    $= (200 \times 3) + (50 \times 1)$
    $= 600 + 50$
    $= 650\ \mu Sv$

    (b) $\dot{H} = \dfrac{H}{t} = 650\ \mu Sv\ year^{-1}$

16. (a) When a radiation detector is used, in the absence of any obvious radioactive sources, it will record a count. This background radiation comes from various sources and is all around us.

    (b) 2.2 mSv

    (c) 1 mSv

17. (a) cosmic radiation; rocks and building materials; gases in the air; food; our bodies

    (b) e.g. medical work; nuclear industry

18. They have greater exposure to cosmic radiation.

Half-life

1. The activity decreases.

2. the time period during which the activity of the source falls to half of its original value

3. The activity of a radioactive source decreases as time goes on and depends on the activity remaining at a particular time. Also the decay of individual atoms is random and unpredictable. However, the time taken for half of the atoms in a radioactive sample to decay is found to be a constant for that source. This time period is the half-life of the source. The half-life of some sources is as low as a fraction of a second; for others it is many thousands of years.

4. The background radiation is first measured. Then the activity of the radioactive source is measured over a suitable period of time. A graph of the activity of the source, corrected for background radiation, is plotted.

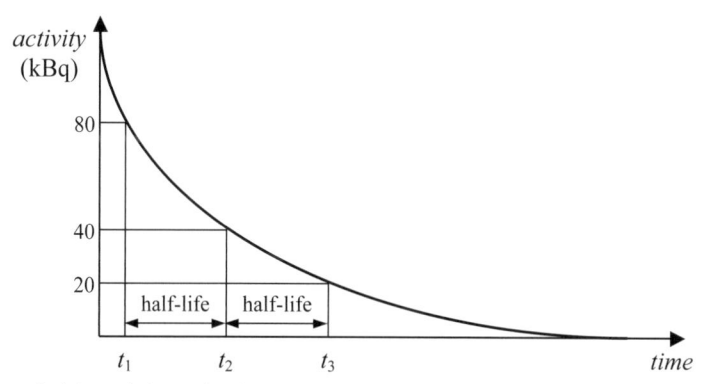

A suitable activity value is chosen, say 80 kBq, and the time at which the source had this activity, t_1, is marked as above. In a similar way the time t_2 at which the activity is half the previous value, 40 kBq, is found. The half-life of the source is the time period $t_2 - t_1$. Any starting value can be chosen, the time period for the activity to half in value will always be the same and is known as the half-life.

5. The half-life of the source is 15 days, so 60 days is equal to 4 half-lives.
   original activity = 1600 kBq
   activity after 1 half-life = $\frac{1}{2} \times 1600$ = 800 kBq
   activity after 2 half-lives = $\frac{1}{2} \times 800$ = 400 kBq
   activity after 3 half-lives = $\frac{1}{2} \times 400$ = 200 kBq
   activity after 4 half-lives = $\frac{1}{2} \times 200$ = 100 kBq

6. original activity = 200 kBq
    activity after 1 half-life = $\frac{1}{2} \times 200$ = 100 kBq
    activity after 2 half-lives = $\frac{1}{2} \times 100$ = 50 kBq
    activity after 3 half-lives = $\frac{1}{2} \times 50$ = 25 kBq
    So 6 years represents 3 half-lives, thus one half-life is 2 years.

7. initial acivity = 120 counts/minute
    activity after 1 half-life = $\frac{1}{2} \times 200$ = 60 counts/minute
    activity after 2 half-lives = $\frac{1}{2} \times 60$ = 30 counts/minute
    activity after 3 half-lives = $\frac{1}{2} \times 30$ = 15 counts/minute

    So 15 counts/minute represents 3 half-lives, i.e. 3×4 = 12 hours.

8. (a)

Week	1	2	3	4	5	6	7	8	9
Recorded activity (counts/minute)	140	82.0	50.0	33.0	23.5	18.0	15.5	14.0	13.0
Corrected activity (counts/minute)	128	70.0	38.0	21.0	11.5	6.0	3.5	2.0	1.0

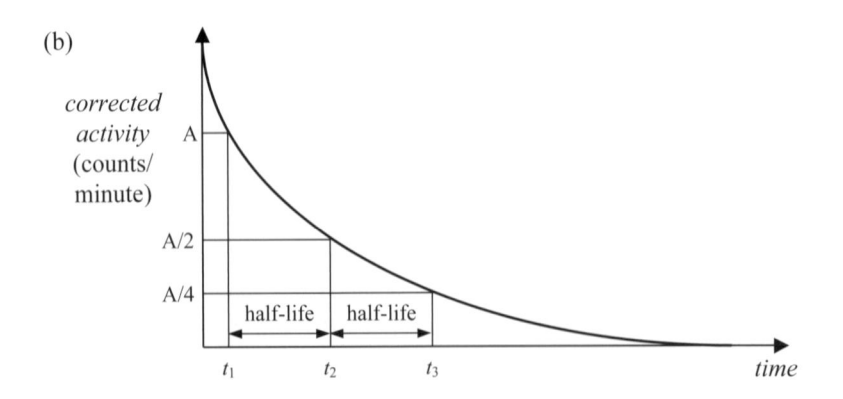

(b)

(c) about 1.15 weeks, or 8 days

Applications of nuclear radiation

1. A Geiger-Müller tube contains a low pressure gas. When any radiation enters the thin mica window it ionises this gas and allows a current between the two electrodes. This means that a Geiger-Müller tube can be used as a radiation detector.

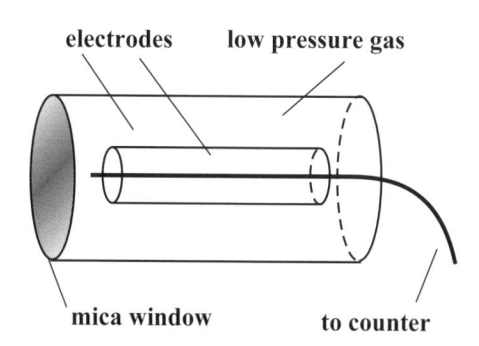

2. The badge contains a small piece of photographic film behind various thicknesses of different absorbers of radiation. When the film is developed, the amount of fogging at each part of it gives an indication of the amount and the intensity of any radiation that the badge and hence the wearer have been exposed to.

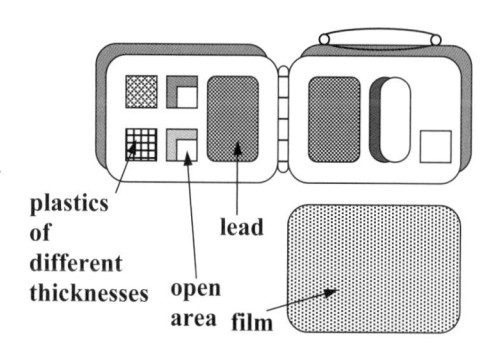

3. (a) a camera that detects gamma radiation

   (b) e.g. to identify and monitor problems in the bones (bone scans)

   (c) The scintillations caused by radiation are made use of in scintillation counters and gamma cameras. Patients are given drugs combined with chemicals which emit gamma radiations. These radiations are detected by a gamma camera which builds up images of internal organs. The gamma radiations cause scintillations when they reach crystals in the camera and these flashes of light in turn produce electrical impulses which are used to build up images of the organs.

4. In a smoke detector, a small sample of the radioactive material americium-241 is used to ionise air particles. These ions flow as an electric current. When there is smoke present, the smoke particles become attached to the ions and this reduces the size of the current. This in turn sets off an audible alarm as a warning.

5. to sterilise instruments (by killing bacteria); to treat cancer

6. (a) a chemical compound that contains radioactive atoms; by tracing the radiation, the movement of the atoms can be followed.

   (b) (i) E.g. in medicine, a tracer is taken into the body either as an injection or as a drink (sometimes called a 'barium meal'). The gamma radiation that it gives off is monitored and gives an indication of any problems there may be in an organ.

   (ii) E.g. in agriculture, it is important to know how well plants make use of fertilisers. To do this, a small amount of the tracer is added to the fertiliser. Its progress through the plant can then be monitored, to give an indication of how the fertiliser is being utilised by the plant.

   (iii) E.g. in industry, tracers can be used to monitor the flow of liquids. Leaks in underground water and sewage pipes can be detected by monitoring the radioactivity in the soil surrounding them. Similarly, by the use of tracers, pollution levels or water flow in rivers can be monitored, using mobile detectors.

7. (a) so that the activity reduces over a short time period

   (b) (i) gamma

   (ii) alpha and beta radiation would not penetrate the body to reach the outside detector (a gamma camera)

8. (a) A radioisotope is placed on one side of a production line and a detector on the other. The reading for the required thickness is set. If the thickness decreases, the reading increases and if the thickness increases the reading decreases and any change leads to automatic adjustment.

   (b) beta

   (c) so that it does not need to be replaced too often

Fission and fusion reactions

1. the process of breaking up the nucleus of an atom into smaller nuclei with the release of energy

2. Induced fission is a result of the bombardment of nuclei by neutrons. Spontaneous fission occurs naturally; this usually happens with larger atomic nuclei.

3. (a) Neutrons are used to bombard the nuclei of atoms. When a neutron is absorbed by a nucleus, the nucleus can become unstable and splits into two smaller nuclei, usually with the release of neutrons. There is loss in mass as a result of the reaction. The difference in mass is converted to energy.

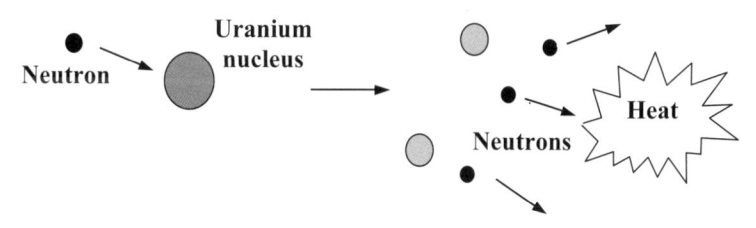

   (b) uranium

4. When the fission of a uranium-235 nucleus takes place, one of the products of the fission reaction is up to three neutrons. If the concentration of uranium-235 nuclei is high enough, each of these neutrons can go on to cause fission of further uranium-235 nuclei. As long as the conditions remain favourable, the neutrons produced continue to cause fission of further nuclei in ever increasing numbers. This type of reaction is called a chain reaction.

   The diagram below shows three stages of such a chain reaction.

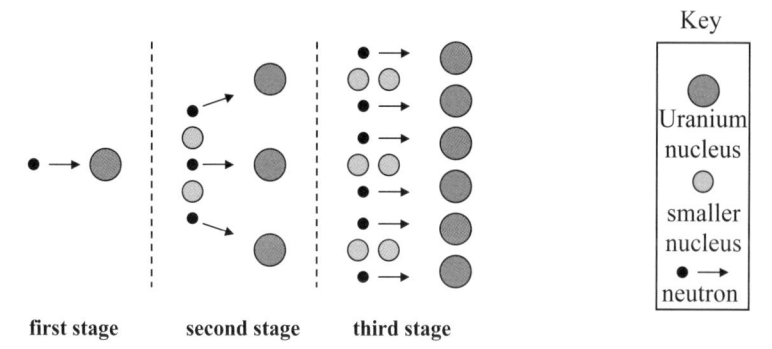

5. The neutrons are slowed down by collisions with the nuclei of another material in the core – the moderator. This material is usually graphite, water or heavy water. Control rods made of boron or carbon are also used. These rods are raised and lowered automatically in response to changes of temperature, sensed by thermistors in the core of the reactor. The material of the control rods absorbs neutrons and so prevents them causing further fission.
    A further set of control rods is normally suspended above the core of the reactor ready to fall into the reactor core in an emergency if the core becomes too hot. When all the control rods are in the core, the reaction is shut down completely.

6. (a) Radioactive waste products still emit radiation which can be harmful.

    (b) (i)   e.g. contaminated gloves

         (ii) E.g. plutonium is a highly radioactive waste product obtained from the uranium fuel used in fission reactors.

    (c) Low level radioactive waste can be disposed of in landfill sites. Being radioactive it is subject to government regulations.
         High level radioactive waste can be reprocessed to obtain further nuclear fuel or it can be encased in glass and buried deep underground, in stable geological formations.

7. the process of joining two nuclei to form a new nucleus of larger mass with a release of energy

8. (a) When a uranium nucleus splits up, the nucleus of atoms of two different **elements** are formed, and **energy** is given out.
         This process is known as nuclear **fission**.

    (b) When two nuclei of low mass combine, the nucleus of an atom of a different **element** is formed, and **energy** is given out.
         This process is known as nuclear **fusion**.

9. (a) Nuclear fusion only takes place at very high temperatures and at very high pressures.

    (b) the fuel used is abundant; there is no danger of a radiation leak above background radiation level; less radioactive waste is produced

Unit 3   Dynamics and Space

Velocity and displacement – vectors and scalars

Vector and scalar quantities

1. (a) A scalar quantity has magnitude (size) only and can be fully described by a number and a unit.

    (b) A vector quantity has magnitude (size) and direction and needs a number, a unit and a direction to describe it fully.

2.

Scalar quantities	Vector quantities
distance	displacement
speed	velocity
energy	force
work done	acceleration
temperature	weight
heat	gravitational field strength
time	
mass	

3. (a) Distance is a scalar quantity that indicates how far an object moves. Displacement is a vector quantity that indicates the distance between two points in a given direction.

    (b) Speed is a scalar quantity that indicates the distance that an object moves in a certain time.
    Velocity is a vector quantity that indicates the displacement of an object in a certain time. Velocity also gives the direction of motion.

4. (a) speed

    (b) velocity

    (c) speed

    (d) velocity

5. (a) 400 m

    (b) 0 m (since the race starts and finishes at the same place)

6. (a) 23 km

    (b) 17 km west

Resultant of vector quantities

1. (a) distance = 200 + 100 = 300 m
    (b) displacement = 200 + 100 = 300 m east

2. (a) distance = 50 + 30 = 80 m
    (b) displacement = 50 – 30 = 20 m south

3. (a) distance = 500 + 500 + 500 = 1500 m
    (b)

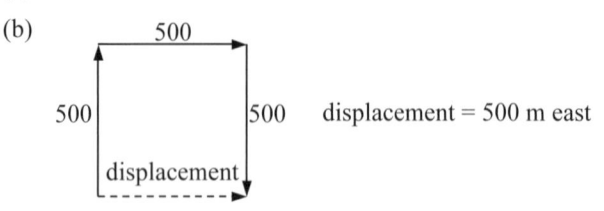

    ```
           500
       ┌────────►
       │        │
    500│        │500    displacement = 500 m east
       │        │
       │displacement
       └ ─ ─ ─ ─►
    ```

4. If the forces acting on an object do not balance each other, then the extra force is called the resultant force. The combined effect of two or more forces acting on an object is the resultant of the forces and is the vector sum of these forces.

5. (a) 3 + 6 = 9 N to the right
    (b) 4 + 8 = 12 N to the left
    (c) 5 – 3 = 2 N to the right
    (d) 3 – 7 = –4 N to the left, or 4 N to the right

6. Resultant velocity
    = velocity of plane w.r.t. air + velocity of plane w.r.t. ground
    = 120 + (-20) m s^{-1} north   = 100 m s^{-1} north

7. (a) [diagram: square with sides 24, 24, diagonal R]

    (b) [diagram: rectangle with sides 8, 6, diagonal R, angle α]

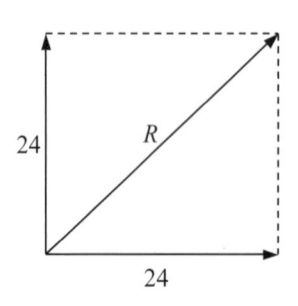

    Resultant, $R = \sqrt{24^2 + 24^2}$
    = 34 N
    at 45° as shown

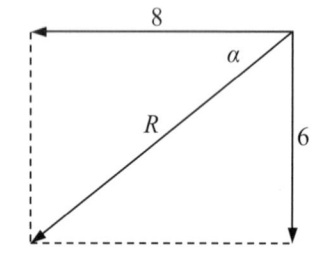

    Resultant, $R = 10$ N
    $\tan\alpha = \frac{6}{8}$ ∴ $\alpha = 37°$
    at 37° as shown

8. A free body diagram shows the forces acting at one point in a system and is used to find the resultant of forces acting on an object.

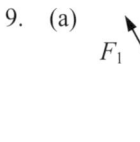

9. (a)

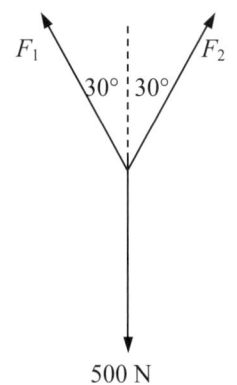

F_1, F_2 at 30° each side of vertical, 500 N downward.

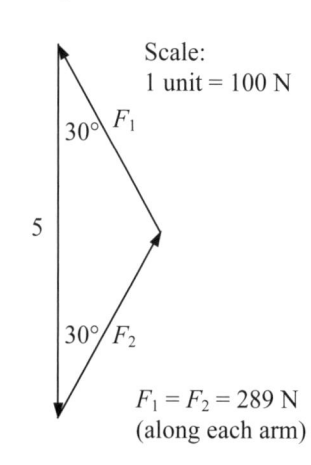

(b) Scale: 1 unit = 100 N

$F_1 = F_2 = 289$ N (along each arm)

10. (a)

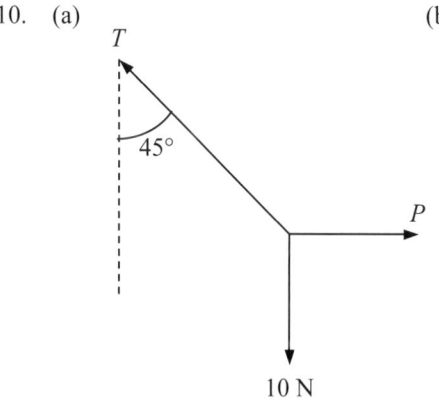

T at 45°, 10 N downward, P horizontal.

(b) 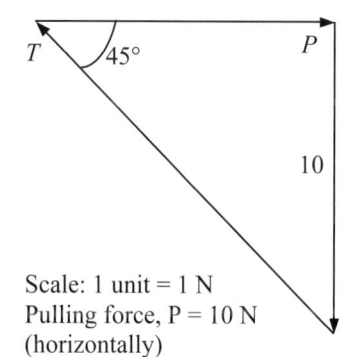 Scale: 1 unit = 1 N
Pulling force, $P = 10$ N (horizontally)

T at 45°, 10 along hypotenuse, P horizontal.

11.

50 000 N upper, 50 000 N lower, R horizontal.

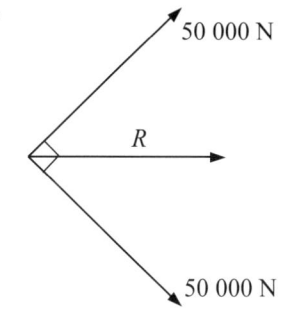

Scale: 1 unit = 10 000 N

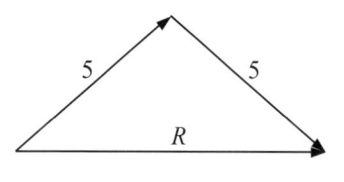

Resultant, $R = 70\,711$ N (direction as shown)

Dynamics and Space Answers

Speed, velocity and time

1. (a) **Speed** is the distance travelled by an object per unit time. Speed does **not** have a direction.

   (b) **Velocity** is the displacement of an object per unit time. Displacement includes the distance and direction of the object in relation to its starting position.

2. (a) $v = \dfrac{d}{t}$

   (b) v is measured in metres per second, m s^{-1}
   d is measured in metres, m
   t is measured in seconds, s

3. $\bar{v} = \dfrac{d}{t}$

4. (a) $\bar{v} = \dfrac{s}{t}$

   (b) v is measured in metres per second, m s^{-1}
   s is displacement measured in metres, m
   t is time measured in seconds, s

5. $\bar{v} = \dfrac{s}{t}$

6. Measure the distance, d, using an appropriate instrument, e.g. a trundle wheel. Record the time, t, it takes the runner to cover the distance using a suitable timing device. For distances greater than about 10 m, a stopwatch is accurate enough. Repeat the timing and find an average of the values.
   The average speed is calculated using: $\bar{v} = \dfrac{d}{t}$

7. displacement, $s = 110$ m
   time, $t = 12.4$ s
   $\bar{v} = \dfrac{s}{t} = \dfrac{110}{12.4} = 8.87$ m s^{-1}

8. distance, $d = 31$ km $= 31\ 000$ m
   average speed, $\bar{v} = 8.1$ m s^{-1}
   $\bar{v} = \dfrac{d}{t} \quad \therefore 8.1 = \dfrac{31\ 000}{t}$ so $t = \dfrac{31\ 000}{8.1} = 3827$ s

   (3800 s to 2 significant figures)

9. distance, $d = 72$ km $= 72\,000$ m
   time, $t = 1\frac{1}{4}$ hours $= 75$ minutes $= 75 \times 60$ s $= 4500$ s
   $$\bar{v} = \frac{d}{t} = \frac{72\,000}{4500} = 16 \text{ m s}^{-1}$$

10. time, $t = 1$ minute $= 60$ s
    speed, $v = 340$ m s^{-1}
    $\bar{v} = \frac{d}{t}$ ∴ $340 = \frac{d}{60}$ so $d = 340 \times 60 = 20\,400$ m, or 20.4 km

11. (a) The instantaneous speed of an object is the speed of the object at a particular point in time.

    (b) the speed recorded on the speedometer of a car; the speed shown on the airspeed indicator of an aeroplane

    (c) One method uses a light gate connected to a timing device such as a computer. The width of the object, or of the mask attached to the object, which interrupts the light beam going to the light gate, is measured. This is the distance, d.
    The object is then allowed to interrupt the light beam and the time, t, for this to happen is recorded on the electronic timing device.
    The instantaneous speed of the object is calculated using: $v = \frac{d}{t}$

12. (a) the time taken for a person to respond to a stimulus, e.g. hearing a sound or seeing something happen, before they are able to do something about it, such as start or stop a stopwatch; reaction time can be as much as half a second or more

    (b) This is because of reaction time. Since the time periods being measured are usually small, often a fraction of a second, a reaction time of up to half a second with a manual stopwatch is very significant, and will give a very inaccurate time measurement.

13. (a) displacement, $s = 30$ km
    time, $t = \frac{1}{2}$ hour
    average velocity $= \frac{\text{total displacement}}{\text{total time}}$ $\bar{v} = \frac{s}{t} = \frac{30}{\frac{1}{2}} = 60$ km h^{-1} east

    (b) The instantaneous velocity will be 0 when the bus is stationary or picking up passengers. It will be 80 km h^{-1} at times on the motorway and will have various values up to the speed limit in town traffic.

    (c) The instantaneous velocity constantly changes, depending on the conditions. The average velocity is calculated over the whole journey, and takes account of varying instantaneous speeds.

14. (a) 15 km, or 15 000 m
    (b) 0 (back at the start)
    (c) distance, $d = 15\,000$ m
    time, $t = 1$ hour 40 minutes $= 100 \times 60$ s
    $$\text{average speed} = \frac{\text{distance}}{\text{time}} = \frac{15\,000}{100 \times 60} = 2.5 \text{ m s}^{-1}$$
    (d) $\bar{v} = 0$ (m s^{-1}), because displacement $= 0$

15. (a) distance, $d = 270$ km
    time, $t = 3$ minutes $= 180$ s
    $$\bar{v} = \frac{d}{t} = \frac{270}{180} = 1.5 \text{ m s}^{-1}$$
    (b) displacement, $s = 180$ m
    time, $t = 3$ minutes $= 180$ s
    $$\bar{v} = \frac{s}{t} = \frac{180}{180} = 1.0 \text{ m s}^{-1} \text{ north}$$

Acceleration

1. Acceleration is the change of velocity in unit time or the rate of change of velocity.

2. (a) a
   (b) the metre per second per second, $m\ s^{-2}$

3. zero, since the rate of change of speed is zero

4. (a) that the object is slowing down
   (b) deceleration

5. the maximum acceleration of a car

6. (a) $a = \dfrac{\Delta v}{t}$
   (b) a is acceleration measured in metres per second per second, $m\ s^{-2}$
   Δv is change in velocity measured in metres per second, $m\ s^{-1}$
   t is time for velocity to change measured in seconds, s

7. $a = \dfrac{v-u}{t}$
   a is acceleration measured in $m\ s^{-2}$
   v is final velocity measured in $m\ s^{-1}$
   u is initial velocity measured in $m\ s^{-1}$
   t is time for velocity to change measured in s

8. $a = \dfrac{v-u}{t}$
   so $v - u = at$ so $v = u + at$

9. change in velocity, $\Delta v = 9.0\ m\ s^{-1}$
   time, $t = 5.0\ s$
   $a = \dfrac{\Delta v}{t} = \dfrac{9.0}{5.0} = 1.8\ m\ s^{-2}$

10. initial velocity, $u = 0$ (from rest)
    final velocity, $v = 28$ m s^{-1}
    time, $t = 8.0$ s

    $$a = \frac{v-u}{t} = \frac{28-0}{8.0} = 3.5 \text{ m s}^{-2}$$

11. acceleration, $a = 0.6$ m s^{-2}
    initial velocity, $u = 2.0$ m s^{-1}
    time, $t = 30$ s

    $$a = \frac{v-u}{t} \quad \therefore 0.6 = \frac{v-2.0}{30}$$

    so $0.6 \times 30 = v - 2.0$ so $v = (0.6 \times 30) + 2.0 = 18 + 2.0 = 20$ m s^{-1}

12. initial velocity, $u = 6.4$ m s^{-1}
    final velocity, $v = 0$ (rest)
    time, $t = 4.0$ s

    $$a = \frac{v-u}{t} = \frac{0-6.4}{4.0} = -1.6 \text{ m s}^{-2} \quad \text{(negative to show deceleration)}$$

13. acceleration, $a = 0.1$ m s^{-2}
    initial velocity, $u = 1$ m s^{-1}
    final velocity, $v = 5$ m s^{-1}

    $$a = \frac{v-u}{t} \quad \therefore 0.1 = \frac{5-1}{t} \quad \text{so } t = \frac{5-1}{0.1} = \frac{4}{0.1} = 40 \text{ s}$$

14. acceleration, $a = -2$ m s^{-2} (deceleration, so negative)
    final velocity, $v = 0$ (rest)
    time, $t = 10$ s

    $$a = \frac{v-u}{t} \quad \therefore -2 = \frac{0-u}{10} \quad \text{so } (-2) \times 10 = 0 - u \quad \text{so } u = 20 \text{ m s}^{-1}$$

Dynamics and Space Answers

Velocity-time graphs

1.

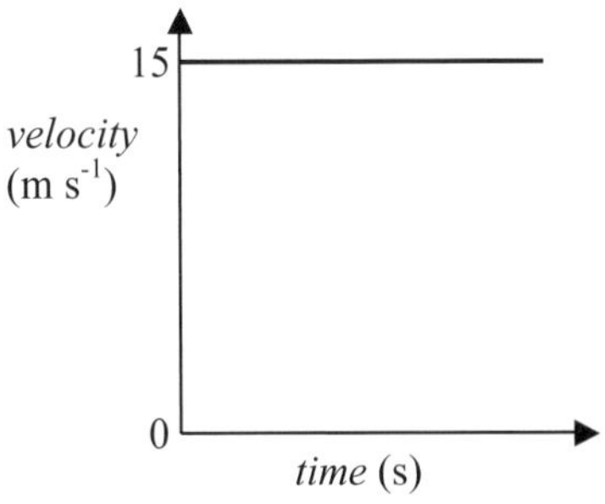

2.

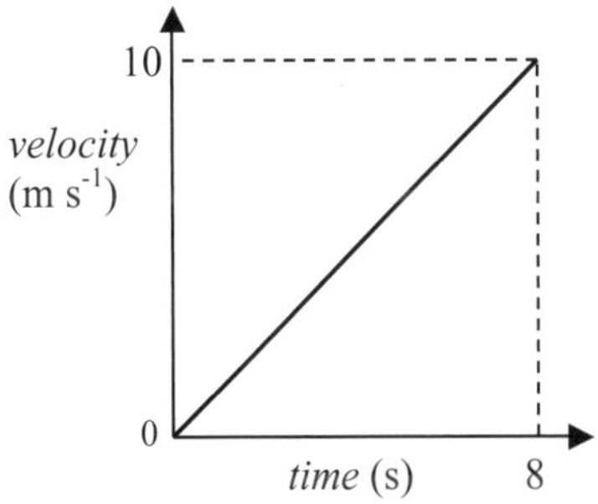

3.

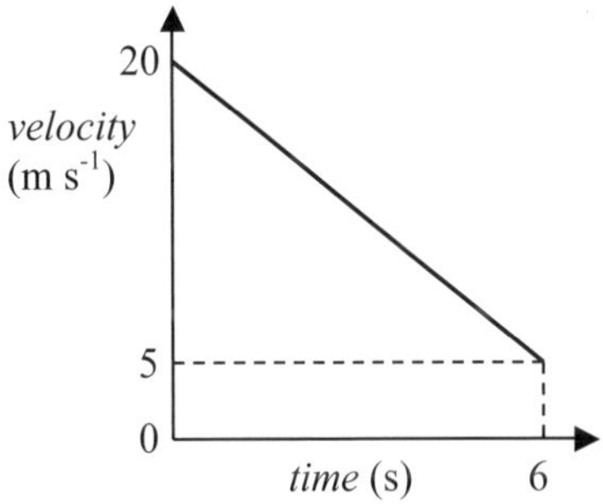

4. Displacement is represented by the area between the graph and the time axis (sometimes referred to as the 'area under the graph').

5. Calculate the gradient of the velocity–time graph.

6. (i) (a) an object travelling at a steady velocity of 20 m s^{-1} for 3 s
   (b) displacement, s = area under graph = $3 \times 20 = 60$ m
   (c) Since the velocity of the object does not change, its acceleration is zero.

   (ii) (a) an object increasing velocity uniformly from 0 to 20 m s^{-1} in 4 s
   (b) displacement, s = area under graph = $\frac{1}{2}(4 \times 20) = 40$ m
   (c) acceleration, $a = \dfrac{v-u}{t} = \dfrac{20-0}{4} = 5$ m s^{-2}

   (iii) (a) an object increasing velocity uniformly from 10 m s^{-1} to 20 m s^{-1} in 2 s
   (b) displacement, $s = (2 \times 10) + \frac{1}{2}[2 \times (20-10)] = 20 + 10 = 30$ m
   (c) acceleration, $a = \dfrac{v-u}{t} = \dfrac{20-10}{2} = 5$ m s^{-2}

   (iv) (a) an object decreasing velocity from 20 m s^{-1} to 0 in 5 s
   (b) displacement, $s = \frac{1}{2}(5 \times 20) = 50$ m
   (c) acceleration, $a = \dfrac{v-u}{t} = \dfrac{0-20}{5} = -4$ m s^{-2}
   This is a negative acceleration or a deceleration.

7. (a) During section **AB** the car increases its velocity uniformly from 0 to 15 m s^{-1} in 3 s.
   During section **BC** the car travels at a steady velocity of 15 m s^{-1} for 5 s.
   During section **CD** the car decreases its velocity uniformly from 15 m s^{-1} to 0 in 6 s.

   (b) 15 m s^{-1}

   (c) (i) The car accelerates during section **AB** of the graph.
   acceleration, $a = \dfrac{v-u}{t} = \dfrac{15-0}{3} = 5$ m s^{-2}

   (ii) The car decelerates during section **CD** of the graph.
   acceleration, $a = \dfrac{v-u}{t} = \dfrac{0-15}{6} = -2.5$ m s^{-2}

   (d) The displacement of the car is equal to the area under the graph.
   displacement, $s = \frac{1}{2}(3 \times 15) + (5 \times 15) + \frac{1}{2}(6 \times 15)$
   $= 22.5 + 75 + 45$
   $= 142.5$ m

8. (a)

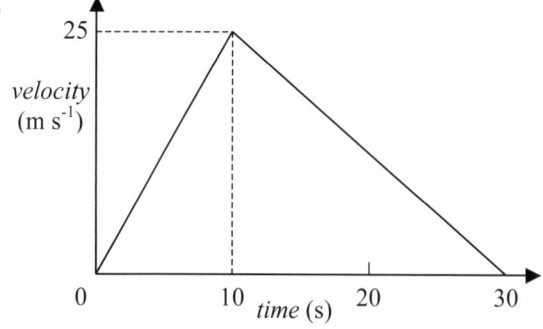

velocity (m s^{-1}) vs time (s): graph rises from (0,0) to (10, 25) then falls to (30, 0).

(b) acceleration, $a = \dfrac{v-u}{t} = \dfrac{25-0}{10} = 2.5 \text{ m s}^{-2}$

(c) deceleration, $a = \dfrac{v-u}{t} = \dfrac{0-25}{20} = -1.25 \text{ m s}^{-2}$

(d) Distance stations are apart is equal to the area under the graph.

distance $= \tfrac{1}{2}(10 \times 25) + \tfrac{1}{2}(20 \times 25)$
$= 125 + 250$
$= 375 \text{ m}$

9. (a)

velocity (m s^{-1}) vs time (s): graph rises from (0,0) to (1, 2) then falls to (3, 0), with dashed lines at velocity 1 and time 1.

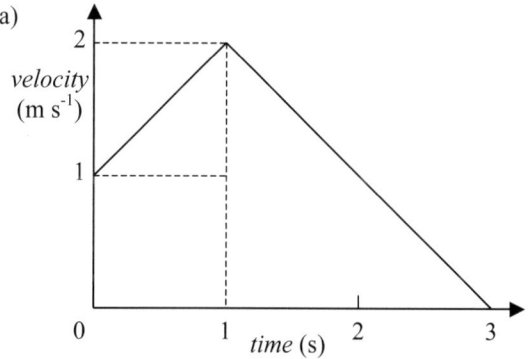

(b) Total length of runway is equal to the area under the graph.

length $= (1 \times 1) + \tfrac{1}{2}(1 \times 1) + \tfrac{1}{2}(2 \times 2)$
$= 1 + \tfrac{1}{2} + 2$
$= 3.5 \text{ m}$

Newton's laws

Force

1. (a) F (b) the newton, N

2. a vector quantity

3. change the shape; change the speed; change the direction of travel

4. (a) A newton balance contains a spring that extends when a force is applied to it. Since the extension is proportional to the force applied to it, a newton balance can be used to measure force.

   (b) to measure force

5. Friction is a force that can oppose the motion of an object.

6. (a) and (b), e.g.
   To slow down a car the brakes are applied. The application of brakes increases the force of friction at the wheels of the car by causing the brake linings to press on the brake drums. This causes the kinetic energy of the car to be converted into heat in the brakes.

   When a parachute is opened the air resistance increases so the increase in speed of the parachute is reduced.

   The grips of rackets and bats used in sports are made of rubber-like material to increase the force of friction between the handle and the hand. This allows a better grip to be maintained.

7. (a) and (b), e.g.
   The force of friction between moving parts in a car engine is reduced by lubricating the moving parts with oil.

   Vehicles are streamlined by making their shape more aerodynamic to reduce the force of friction due to air resistance.

   When skiing, the low value of the force of friction between snow or ice and the ski is reduced even more by making the ski surface as smooth as possible by waxing it.

Balanced forces and Newton's first law

1. Balanced forces are equal forces acting in opposite directions on an object; balanced forces are equivalent to no force at all.

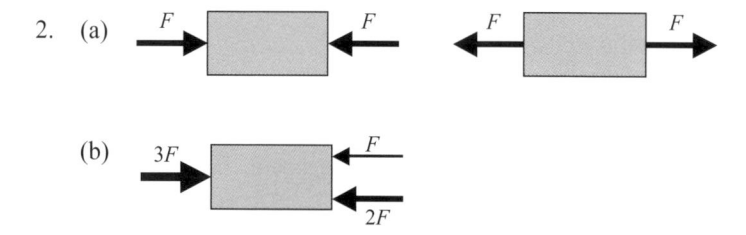

2. (a) $F \rightarrow \boxed{} \leftarrow F \qquad F \leftarrow \boxed{} \rightarrow F$

   (b) $3F \rightarrow \boxed{} \leftarrow F$, $2F \downarrow$

3. Since the block of wood is not moving, its speed is constant (zero) and so the forces acting on it are balanced.

4. (a) The forces are balanced.

   (b) The engine has to supply a force to balance the force of friction trying to slow it down.

5. A force has to be supplied to balance the force of friction trying to slow the bicycle down.

6. An object will continue in its state of rest or of uniform motion unless it is acted upon by an external, unbalanced force.

7. (a) The velocity stays the same.

   (b) The velocity stays the same.

8. (a) The forces acting on it are balanced. Since there are no unbalanced forces acting on it, the book will remain stationary.

   (b) There are no unbalanced forces acting on it. For this to happen the force of friction that is present when the car moves must be balanced by the force supplied by the engine.

   (c) The spaceship is in a situation where there are no forces acting on it, so once it is moving it will continue at the same speed in the same direction.

9. (a) to supply a restraining force to stop the continued forward motion of the occupant when the car stops suddenly

   (b) If a car stops suddenly, an unrestrained occupant would continue to move forward at the same original speed and would probably hit the windscreen. A seat belt provides a backward force to reduce this speed in line with the reduced speed of the car.

Dynamics and Space Answers

Unbalanced force and Newton's Second Law

1. An unbalanced force causes an object to accelerate.

2. (a) The acceleration of the object increases.
   (b) The acceleration of the object increases.

3. The car will accelerate.

4. When a second person jumps on to a moving skateboard, the mass increases and so its acceleration decreases, if the unbalanced force remains the same.

5. The mass of the balloon is decreased. As a result, the weight also decreases. The upward air resistance is now greater than the downward weight causing an upward unbalanced force. Both of these effects cause the balloon to have an upward acceleration.

6. The mass of an object is the amount of matter that the object contains.

7. (a) m (b) the kilogram, kg

8. (a) $a = \dfrac{F}{m}$

   (b) a is acceleration measured in metres per second per second, m s^{-2}
   F is unbalanced force measured in newtons, N
   m is mass measured in kilograms, kg

9. The newton is defined in terms of the acceleration produced in an object by an unbalanced (or resultant force). The newton is the force that causes an object of mass 1 kg to have an acceleration of 1 m s^{-2}.

10. The acceleration produced in an object is directly proportional to the unbalanced force acting on it and inversely proportional to its mass.

11. mass, $m = 0.75$ kg
    unbalanced force, $F = 3.0$ N
    $a = \dfrac{F}{m} = \dfrac{3.0}{0.75} = 4$ m s^{-2}

12. acceleration, $a = 5$ m s^{-2}
    mass, $m = 2$ kg
    $a = \dfrac{F}{m} \quad \therefore 5 = \dfrac{F}{2} \quad$ so $F = 5 \times 2 = 10$ N

13. unbalanced force, $F = -1500$ N
    acceleration, $a = -2.40$ m s^{-2}
    $$a = \frac{F}{m} \quad \therefore -2.40 = \frac{-1500}{m} \quad \text{so } m = \frac{-1500}{-2.40} = 625 \text{ kg}$$

14. mass, $m = 1200$ kg
    driving force = 2500 N
    resistive forces = 700 N

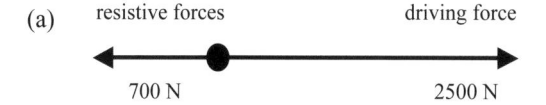

    (a)

    resistive forces   driving force

    ←—————●—————→

    700 N   2500 N

    (b) unbalanced force, $F = (2500 - 700) = 1800$ N
    $$a = \frac{F}{m} = \frac{1800}{1200} = 1.5 \text{ m s}^{-2}$$

15. mass, $m = 120$ kg
    acceleration, $a = 0.10$ m s^{-2} downwards
    $$a = \frac{F}{m} \quad \therefore 0.1 = \frac{F}{120} \quad \text{so } F = 0.1 \times 120 = 12 \text{ N downwards}$$

Work done, force and distance/displacement

1. When an object is moved, the amount of work that is done is a measure of the **energy** transferred.

2. (a) E
   (b) the joule, J
   (c) E_w or W

3. (a) $E_w = Fd$
   (b) E_w (or W) is work done (energy transferred) measured in joules, J
       F is unbalanced force measured in newtons, N
       d is distance measured in metres, m

4. force, $F = 5.0$ N
   distance, $d = 3.0$ m
   $$E_w = Fd = 5.0 \times 3.0 = 15 \text{ J}$$

Dynamics and Space Answers

5. energy (work done), $E_w = 1197$ J
   distance, $d = 21$ m

   $E_w = Fd \quad \therefore 1197 = F \times 21 \quad \text{so } F = \dfrac{1197}{21} = 57$ N

6. energy (work done), $E_w = 210$ J
   force, $F = 50$ N

   $E_w = Fd \quad \therefore 210 = 50 \times d \quad \text{so } d = \dfrac{210}{50} = 4.2$ m

7. (a) $P = \dfrac{E_w}{t}$

   (b) P is power measured in watts, W
   E is work done (energy transferred) measured in joules, J
   t is time measured in seconds, s

8. energy, $E = 360$ J
   time, $t = 1$ minute $= 60$ s

   $P = \dfrac{E}{t} = \dfrac{360}{60} = 6$ W

9. (a) $P = \dfrac{E_w}{t}$ and $E_w = F \times d$ so $P = \dfrac{F \times d}{t}$

   (b) $P = \dfrac{F \times d}{t}$ but $\dfrac{d}{t} = v$ so $P = F \times v$

10. mass, $m = 0.3$ kg
    acceleration due to gravity, $g = 9.8$ m s^{-2}
    speed, $v = 20$ cm s^{-1} $= 0.2$ m s^{-1}

    $P = F \times v =$ weight x $v = 0.3 \times 9.8 \times 0.2 = 0.588$ W
    (0.6 to 2 significant figures)

11. gravitational potential energy

12. The work done against gravity is equal to the increase in **gravitational potential energy** of an object.

13. when the object moves to a lower position or loses height

14. mass, $m = 61$ kg
 height, $h = 25$ m
 time, $t = 1$ minute $= 60$ s
 acceleration due to gravity, $g = 9.8$ m s^{-2}

 (a) $E_p = mgh = 61 \times 9.8 \times 25 = 14\ 945$ J

 (15 000 J, or 15 kJ to 2 significant figures)

 (b) $P = \dfrac{E}{t} = \dfrac{14\ 945}{60} = 249$ W (250 W to 2 significant figures)

 (c) If the crate falls, all of its potential energy will be transformed into kinetic energy.

 $$E_k = \tfrac{1}{2}mv^2$$
 $$\therefore 14\ 945 = \tfrac{1}{2} \times 61 \times v^2$$
 $$\therefore v^2 = \dfrac{14\ 945 \times 2}{61}$$
 $$\therefore v = 22\text{ m s}^{-1}$$

Gravitational field strength

1. the pull of the Earth or another planet on the mass of the object

2. (a) W
   (b) the newton, N

3. (a) the force of gravity
   (b) All objects have the same acceleration (if the effects of friction can be ignored).

4. 9.8 m s^{-2}

5. the region round about a planet or a star where it exerts a pull on any object which has a mass

6. the ratio of weight to mass, or the weight per unit mass

7. 9.8 N kg^{-1}

8. Mass is the amount of 'stuff' or matter that an object contains.
   Weight is the pull of the Earth or other body on this matter. For any object, the mass remains constant but the weight can vary since it depends on the gravitational field strength.

9. (a) $W = mg$
   (b) W is weight measured in newtons, N
   m is mass measured in kilograms, kg
   g is gravitational field strength measured in newtons per kilogram, N kg^{-1}; this unit is also equal to the metre per second per second, m s^{-2}

10. Gravitational field strength, g, is weight per unit mass: $g = \dfrac{W}{m}$
    An object free to move in a gravitational field will accelerate because of the resultant (unbalanced) force acting on it, called its weight, obeying Newton's Second Law.
    $W = ma$ (a is the acceleration due to gravity)
    Combining these equations gives
    $$g = \frac{W}{m} = \frac{ma}{m} = a$$
    gravitational field strength = acceleration due to gravity
    The units of both quantities, N kg^{-1} and m s^{-2}, are also equivalent.

11. 9.8 N kg^{-1}

12. mass, $m = 52$ kg
    gravitational field strength, $g = 9.8 \text{ N kg}^{-1}$
    $W = mg = 52 \times 9.8 = 509.6$ N   (510 N to 2 significant figures)

13. mass, $m = 1$ kg
    gravitational field strength, $g = 9.8 \text{ N kg}^{-1}$
    $W = mg = 1 \times 9.8 = 9.8$ N   (10 N to 1 significant figure)

14. weight, $W = 98\,000$ N
    gravitational field strength, $g = 9.8 \text{ N kg}^{-1}$
    $W = mg$ $\therefore 98000 = m \times 9.8$ so $m = \dfrac{98000}{9.8} = 10\,000$ kg

15. mass, $m = 58$ kg
    time, $t = 9.0$ s
    height, $h = 5.1$ m
    gravitational field strength, $g = 9.8 \text{ N kg}^{-1}$

    (a) $W = mg = 58 \times 9.8 = 568.4$ N   (570 N to 2 significant figures)

    (b) $E_w = Fd =$ weight x height $= 568.4 \times 5.1 = 2899$ J
    (2900 J to 2 significant figures)

    (c) $P = \dfrac{E}{t} = \dfrac{2899}{9.0} = 322$ W   (320 W to 2 significant figures)

16. (a) If the block was taken to the Moon where the gravitational field strength is 1.6 N kg^{-1} its mass would be **unchanged** and its weight would be **decreased**.

    (b) If the block was taken to Jupiter where the gravitational field strength is 23 N kg^{-1} its mass would be **unchanged** and its weight would be **increased**.

    (c) If the block was taken into space, far away from any planets, its mass would be **unchanged** and its weight would be **zero**.

Dynamics and Space Answers

17.

Planet	Gravitational field strength (N kg⁻¹)	Total Weight (N)
Venus	8.9	mg = 122 x 8.9 = 1100
Earth	9.8	mg = 122 x 9.8 = 1200
Mars	3.7	mg = 122 x 3.7 = 450
Jupiter	23.0	mg = 122 x 23.0 = 2800

18. weight on Earth, $W_E = 25$ N
    gravitational field strength on Earth, $g_E = 9.8$ N kg⁻¹
    $W_E = mg$ ∴ $25 = m \times 9.8$ so $m = \dfrac{25}{9.8} = 2.55$ kg
    gravitational field strength on Moon, $g_M = 1.6$ N kg⁻¹
    so weight on Moon $= mg_M = 2.55 \times 1.6 = 4.1$ N

19. when it is out in space far away from all gravitational fields due to planets or stars

20. When an object is falling freely near the surface of the Earth. Free-fall is also experienced by astronauts and their spacecraft when they are orbiting a planet since they are falling freely towards the planet while orbiting.

21. (a) The amount of matter in an object is known as its **mass**.

    (b) The force of gravity acting on an object is known as its **weight**.

    (c) Any object which has a mass also has a reluctance to have its motion changed. This property is known as its **inertia**.

    (d) The ratio of weight to mass for an object close to the surface of a planet is known as that planet's **gravitational field strength**.

    (e) Although they have different units, two quantities are equivalent to each other. These quantities are gravitational field strength and **acceleration due to gravity**.

22. The weight decreases.

23. the force supplied by an engine

24. thrust, $F = 2 \times 10^3$ N $= 2000$ N
    mass, $m = 5 \times 10^3$ kg $= 5000$ kg
    $F = ma$ ∴ $2000 = 5000 \times a$ so $a = \dfrac{2000}{5000} = 0.4$ m s⁻²

Dynamics and Space Answers

25. (a) There is no wind or air resistance since space is a vacuum and there is no gravitational pull from any planet. Since there are no forces acting on the rocket, it will continue to move in a straight line at a steady speed. This is an example of Newton's First Law.

(b) There would be an unbalanced force acting on the rocket and so it would accelerate - either change its speed or change its direction.

26. (a) the constant velocity reached by an object in free-fall

(b) Air resistance increases as velocity increases. An object that is dropped increases its velocity until the downward force of its weight is equal to the upward force of the air resistance acting on it. At this point, it falls with terminal velocity.

27. Air resistance increases as velocity increases. A parachute increases the air resistance, so with a parachute the forces are balanced at a lower terminal velocity.

Newton's third law

1. The propellant gas is pushed back.

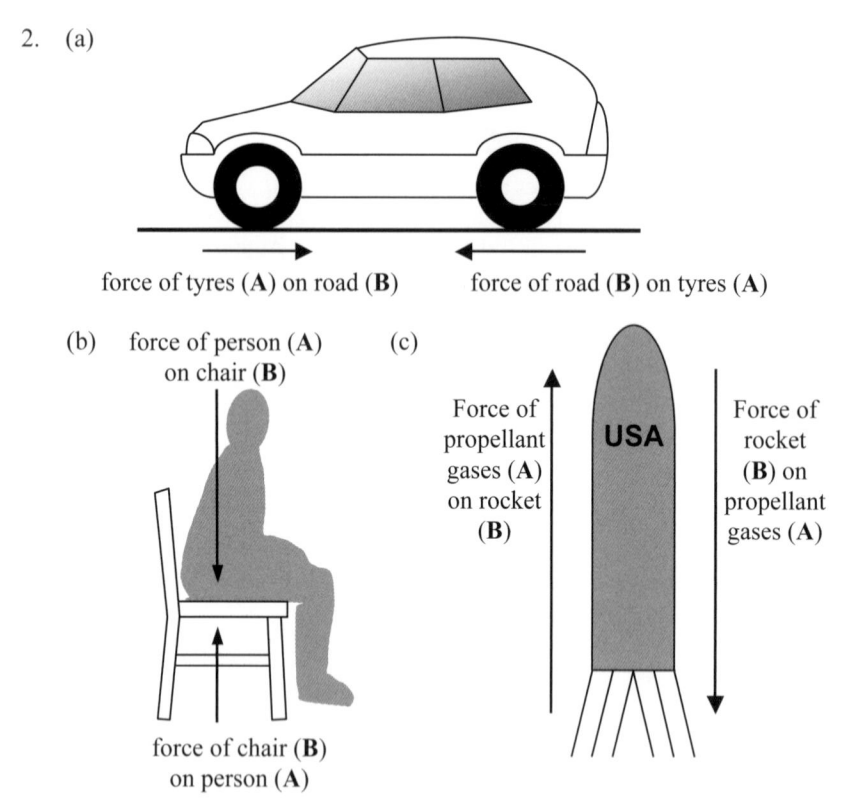

2. (a) force of tyres (**A**) on road (**B**)   force of road (**B**) on tyres (**A**)

   (b) force of person (**A**) on chair (**B**)
       force of chair (**B**) on person (**A**)

   (c) Force of propellant gases (**A**) on rocket (**B**)
       Force of rocket (**B**) on propellant gases (**A**)

3. If **A** exerts a force on **B**, **B** exerts an equal but opposite force on **A**. This law is sometimes quoted as 'action and reaction are equal but opposite'.

4. The two equal but opposite forces which act on each of the two objects **A** and **B** which are mentioned in Newton's Third Law.

5. **Upthrust**: The force of the rotors (**A**) on the air (**B**) and the force of the air (**B**) on the rotors (**A**).
   Weight: The force of the Earth (**A**) on the helicopter (**B**) and the force of the helicopter (**B**) on the Earth (**A**).
   Engine force: The force of the engines (**A**) on the expelled gases (**B**) and the force of the expelled gases (**B**) on the engines (**A**).
   Resistive force: The force of friction of the air (**A**) on the helicopter (**B**) and the force of the helicopter (**B**) on the air (**A**).

6. **Upthrust**: The force of the water (**A**) on the boat (**B**) and the force of the boat (**B**) on the water (**A**).
Weight: The force of the Earth (**A**) on the boat (**B**) and the force of the boat (**B**) on the Earth (**A**).
Force on sail: The force of the air (**A**) on the sail (**B**) and the force of the sail (**B**) on the air (**A**).
Resistive force: The force of friction of the water (**A**) on the boat (**B**) and the force of the boat (**B**) on the water (**A**).

7. Balanced forces act on the same object while "Newton Pairs" act on different objects which interact.
Consider a box sitting on a table:
If the box is at rest, the weight of the box is balanced by the force supplied by the table. Both of these forces act on the box.
The force of the Earth (weight) on the box and the force of the box on the Earth form a "Newton Pair", acting on the box and the Earth respectively. The force of the table on the box and the force of the box on the table form a second "Newton Pair" acting on the box and the table respectively.

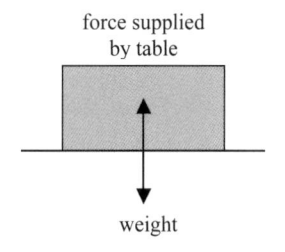

Projectile motion

1. (a) The object follows a curved (parabolic) path.
    (b) The force of gravity accelerates it in the downward (vertical) direction, while it travels forwards (horizontally) at a constant speed.

2. (a) The horizontal motion shows constant speed because no forces act on the projectile horizontally (ignoring air resistance). The horizontal motion of a projectile is governed by Newton's First Law.
    (b) The vertical motion shows uniform acceleration, caused by gravity. The vertical acceleration of a projectile near the Earth's surface is 9.8 m s^{-2}. The vertical motion of a projectile is governed by Newton's Second Law.

3. the time of flight

4. (a) Since the horizontal speed of a projectile is constant, the horizontal speed of the parcel just before it reaches the ground is 55 m s^{-1}.
    (b) horizontally: speed, $v = 55$ m s^{-1}; time, $t = 4.0$ s
    $$v = \frac{d}{t} \therefore 55 = \frac{d}{4.0} \text{ so } d = 55 \times 4.0 = 220 \text{ m}$$
    (c) vertically: $u = 0$ (the parcel starts out with horizontal motion only)
    $a = 9.8$ m s^{-2} (the acceleration due to gravity)
    $t = 4.0$ s (the time is common to horizontal and vertical motions)
    $v = u + at = 0 + (9.8 \times 4.0) = 39.2$ m s^{-1} (39 m s^{-1} to 2 significant figures)
    (d) Sketch the graph of the vertical speed of the parcel against time.
    The height of the helicopter is given by the area under the graph.
    height $= \frac{1}{2}(4.0 \times 39.2) = 78.4$ m (78 m to 2 significant figures)

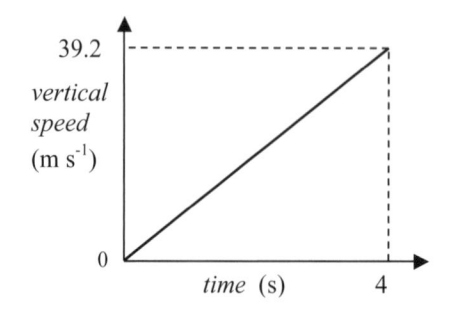

5. A satellite is constantly falling towards the Earth. However, the forward speed of a satellite is so great that because of the curvature of the Earth, the Earth's surface drops away as much as the satellite falls towards it. So the satellite always stays at the same height above the Earth's surface.

6. Long before artificial satellites were put into orbit, Sir Isaac Newton used projectile motion to explain the orbit of satellites in his famous thought experiment. He suggested that a large cannon, fired horizontally from the top of a tall mountain, would have a very large range – well beyond the horizon. He extended the idea to an even taller mountain and an even bigger cannon and suggested that, if it were to fire a shell with a great enough velocity, the shell would always fall towards the Earth but would never reach it. In effect the shell would orbit the Earth because of gravity and would become an artificial satellite.

Space exploration

Our understanding of the universe and planet Earth

1. (a) e.g. our perspective of ourselves and the Earth; our understanding of asteroid strikes; our understanding of exoplanets; our understanding of the age and origins of the universe

    (b) telescopes; space exploration

2. (a) It is not only light that comes to Earth from space. Signals of different wavelengths and frequencies, and so different types of radiation, come to Earth from space.

    (b) reflecting light telescopes; refracting light telescopes; radio telescopes; X-ray telescopes; gamma ray telescopes; infrared telescopes; ultraviolet telescopes

3. e.g. better weather forecasting; finding Earth's resources; environmental research; studying Earth's atmosphere; images to show changes due to natural events/human activity; mapping the Earth; wildlife tracking and preservation; conservation of natural resources

4. (a) Weather satellites show conditions throughout Earth's atmosphere, including the air quality. Satellites record a range of important information including particles in the atmosphere from both natural sources and human activities such as factories, fires, deserts, and erupting volcanoes. Atmospheric gases - ozone, carbon dioxide and other greenhouse gases - are constantly monitored.

    (b) Many scientists think that small changes visible on the Sun's surface can affect weather on Earth. These changes may have caused periods of cooling in Earth's atmosphere. NASA has set up a collection of satellites called the Earth Observation System to "monitor the state of the climate, atmospheric chemistry, ocean and land ecosystems".

    (c) Since the Sun's energy is unaffected in space by the 24-hour cycle of night and day, weather, seasons, or the filtering effect of Earth's atmospheric gases, scientists are working on putting solar panels in orbit and beaming the energy down for use on Earth. This involves wireless power transmission, which could be performed using microwave beams. Scientists and researchers all over the world are trying to harness the power of nuclear fusion – the process which enables the Sun to produce energy. One of the sources they are looking at is helium-3 but there is not enough helium-3 on Earth. However, scientists estimate that the Moon contains more than 1 million tons of the isotope and may be able to exploit it.

(d) Earth's temperature allows liquid water to remain on the surface. Mars and Venus, the planets closest to Earth, have no liquid water on their surfaces. By comparing Earth with those planets, we can see how liquid water has affected the development of Earth's atmosphere. Observations of the Moon and other bodies in space helped scientists understand how gravity works.
Spacecraft have been sent to take close-up pictures of Saturn's rings.
It is thought that an asteroid strike wiped out dinosaurs on Earth. One of the benefits of space exploration is that we know about thousands of asteroids and we can also watch their movement.

5. Minerals buried deep under the Earth's surface can be located using satellites. Fossil fuels can also be found with the help of satellites. These areas have now become potentially rich resources for the country in which they are located.

6. (a) e.g. CAT Scans; voice-controlled wheelchairs; tiny transmitters to monitor the foetus inside the womb; miniaturized heart pumps; programmable pacemakers; cool suits to lower body temperature in the treatment of various conditions; bone-density measurement technology; implantable insulin pumps

(b) e.g ultra-small electronic circuits; the mobile phone camera; scratch-resistant lenses; water filtration and purification systems; aviation safety systems; clean energy technology; fire-resistant materials; protective suits for fire-fighters made from fabric originally used in space suits; materials to endure extreme heat and cold

(c) e.g. better prediction of crop yields; information about pest infestation; a complete geographical analysis of cultivated areas

7. (a) Remote sensing via satellite is widely used to track wildlife. Satellites track many species of marine life including whales, sharks, birds, squid, sea turtles and fish. Satellite data has revealed migration patterns, feeding grounds, behaviour, and ocean deserts.
Antelopes, bears, big cats and parrots are some of the land species whose movements are tracked using satellites. A conservation group has fitted elephants with GPS-enabled collars, allowing researchers to track African elephants as they move through the bush in Kenya.
Satellite images are used by biologists and conservationists who need a bird's eye view of remote and hard to reach areas to monitor wildlife and marine environment activities and operations. These images are used to map habitats and vegetation; to monitor and analyse conservation activities; to study ecological patterns and to monitor wildlife and marine populations and protected wildlife parks. Satellite images help marine conservationists to understand ecosystem changes in critical and protected areas around the world.

(b) Images and data from weather satellites have greatly improved weather forecasting. Scientists can now provide warnings of dangerous storms long before they strike populated areas.
Satellites monitor atmospheric gases (including greenhouse gases) and particles from both natural sources and human activities such as factories, fires, deserts, and erupting volcanoes; energy radiated from Earth's surface and the Sun; ocean surface temperature changes; global sea level; the extent of ice sheets; glaciers and sea ice; plant growth; rainfall; cloud structure; and more.

8. e.g. floods; storms; tornadoes; hurricanes; wildfires

9. (a) kinetic energy

   (b) (i) kinetic to heat

      (ii) the friction as the spacecraft moves quickly through the Earth's atmosphere

10. (a) e.g. a fuel leakage or fire; a part of the craft breaking off

    (b) e.g. effect of cosmic radiation; loss of oxygen; low temperature

    (c) (i) There is immense heat generated due to the force of friction caused by air resistance.

       (ii) e.g. use of heat shield to dissipate energy; loss of uninhabited part of the craft

    (d) e.g. craft not landing in the correct place

Calculations

1. mass, $m = 72\,000$ kg
   speed in orbit, $v = 8500$ m s^{-1}
   speed at touchdown, $v = 94$ m s^{-1}

   (a) kinetic energy of the orbiter while it is in orbit:
   $E_k = \tfrac{1}{2}mv^2 = \tfrac{1}{2} \times 72\,000 \times 8500^2 = 2.6 \times 10^{12}$ J

   (b) kinetic energy of the orbiter just as it touches down:
   $E_k = \tfrac{1}{2}mv^2 = \tfrac{1}{2} \times 72\,000 \times 94^2 = 3.2 \times 10^8$ J

   (c) It has been converted into heat, because the orbiter has been slowed down by friction as it entered the Earth's atmosphere.

   (d) average force needed to stop the orbiter = 180 kN, or 180 000 N
   work done in stopping orbiter, E_W = kinetic energy at touchdown, E_k

   $E_w = Fd \quad \therefore 3.2 \times 10^8 = 180\,000 \times d \quad \text{so } d = \dfrac{3.2 \times 10^8}{180\,000}$
   $= 1767$ m

   (1800 m, or 1.8 km, to 2 significant figures)

2. mass, $m = 3.0$ kg
   speed, $v = 2000$ m s^{-1}
   specific heat capacity of iron, $c = 480$ J kg^{-1}
   kinetic energy, $E_k = \tfrac{1}{2}mv^2 = \tfrac{1}{2} \times 3.0 \times 2000^2 = 6 \times 10^6$ J
   if 10 % of the kinetic energy is converted into heat, then:
   $E_h = E_k \times 10\% = 6 \times 10^5$ J

   $E_h = cm\Delta T \quad \therefore 6 \times 10^5 = 480 \times 3.0 \times \Delta T \quad \text{so } \Delta T = \dfrac{6 \times 10^5}{480 \times 3.0}$
   $= 417\,°C$

   (420 °C to 2 significant figures)

Satellites

1. an object in space that orbits around a bigger object

2. the Moon

3. A low Earth orbit is an orbit around Earth with a height between 160 kilometres and 2000 kilometres.
A polar orbit is one in which a satellite passes above or nearly above both poles of the Earth on each revolution.
A geostationary orbit is a circular orbit 35,786 kilometres above the equator and following the direction of the Earth's rotation. A satellite in such an orbit has a period of one day and so appears to be motionless at a fixed position in the sky.

4.

Type of orbit	Function of satellite
low Earth orbit	Earth observation satellite
	spy satellite
polar orbit	Earth observation satellite
	weather satellite
geostationary orbit	communications satellite
	weather satellite

5. (a) the time it takes for the satellite to make one orbit or revolution round the Earth
   (b) the height of its orbit above the Earth

6. approximately 1000 km

7. because of the curvature of the Earth, since radio waves travel in straight lines

8. Signals from a ground transmitting station are sent to a geostationary satellite. The satellite then boosts and re–transmits the signal to a ground station in the receiving country. A group of three geostationary satellites is sufficient to allow communication right round the world from continent to continent.

9. (a) to make the received signal stronger

   (b) The curved reflector on a receiver collects the signals from a larger area and reflects them to a focus. The aerial is positioned at the focus. The larger the reflector then the stronger is the signal directed to the aerial.

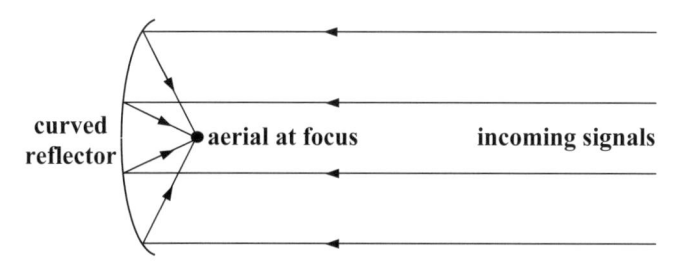

   curved reflector → aerial at focus   incoming signals

10. Signals from satellites are received at the aerial of a ground station that then transmits microwave signals close to the Earth's surface. Since microwaves can only travel a few kilometres they are sent to repeater stations where boosters amplify the signals and re-transmit them.

11. Curved reflectors are used with some transmitters to produce a parallel beam of waves for transmission. They do this because the transmitting aerial is placed at the focus of the curved reflector.

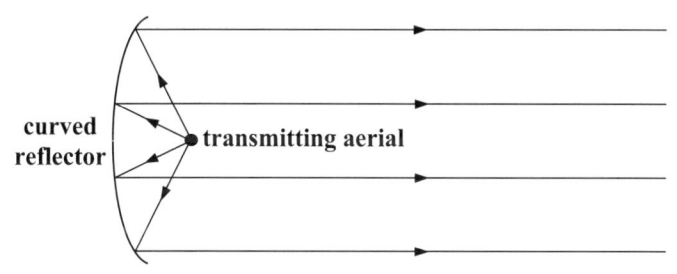

   curved reflector → transmitting aerial

12. distance, $d = 1500$ km $= 1500 \times 10^3$ m

    speed, $v = 3 \times 10^8$ m s^{-1}

    $v = \dfrac{d}{t}$ $\therefore 3 \times 10^8 = \dfrac{1500 \times 10^3}{t}$ so $t = \dfrac{1500 \times 10^3}{3 \times 10^8} = 0.005$ s or 5 ms

Changes in state

1. solid, liquid, gas

2. (a) The temperature of the object can increase, or it can change its state.
   (b) If heat is transferred to an object that is at its melting point or its boiling point already, its state will change; otherwise, its temperature will increase.

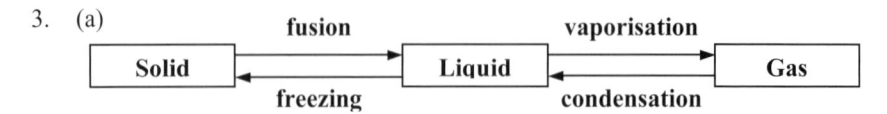

3. (a)

   | Solid | ⇌ fusion / freezing | Liquid | ⇌ vaporisation / condensation | Gas |

   (b) the temperature of the substance

4. (a) heat
   (b) heat

5. (a) and (b) e.g.
   In a refrigerator, a liquid with a low boiling point (originally freon but now replaced by ozone-friendly chemicals) is forced through a narrow valve. As it does so, it is changed into a gas, taking the heat to do so from the contents of the food compartment inside the refrigerator so cooling them down. When it moves outside the cabinet, it is passed through a compressor where it is converted back into a liquid. At this stage it gives up its latent heat and this is convected away from the back of the refrigerator.

   The picnic box cooler is a sealed plastic pack which contains a chemical that can readily be solidified by removing its latent heat of fusion by placing it for some time in a refrigerator. When placed near the top of a cool box, the chemical gradually converts into a liquid again by taking heat from the cool box contents, so keeping them cool.

6. (a) hidden
   (b) The term describes heat that cannot be 'seen' or recorded on a thermometer as a change in temperature.

7. (a) melting
   (b) evaporation

8. (a) the amount of heat needed to change unit mass of the substance from a solid to a liquid, or the heat given out when unit mass of the substance changes from a liquid to a solid

(b) the amount of heat needed to change unit mass of the substance from a liquid to a gas, or the heat given out when unit mass of the substance changes from a gas to a liquid

9. (a) $E_h = ml$

(b) E_h is heat measured in joules, J
 m is mass measured in kilograms, kg
 l is specific latent heat measured in joules per kilogram, J kg^{-1}

10. mass, $m = 0.500$ kg
 specific latent heat of vaporisation of water, $l = 22.60 \times 10^5$ J kg^{-1}
 $E_h = ml = 0.500 \times 22.60 \times 10^5 = 1.13 \times 10^6$ J

11. mass, $m = 0.500$ kg
 specific latent heat of fusion of water, $l = 3.34 \times 10^5$ J kg^{-1}
 $E_h = ml = 0.500 \times 3.34 \times 10^5 = 1.67 \times 10^5$ J

12. (a) 330 °C

(b) mass, $m = 0.44$ kg
 heat energy supplied, $E_h = 1.1 \times 10^4$ J

$E_h = ml$

$1.1 \times 10^4 = 0.44 \times l$

$\therefore l = \dfrac{1.1 \times 10^4}{0.44} = 2.5 \times 10^4$ J kg^{-1}

13. Total heat needed
 = heat to increase temperature of ice from −18 °C to 0 °C = $(cm\Delta T)_{ice}$
 + heat to melt ice to water at 0 °C = $(ml)_{fusion\ of\ ice}$
 + heat to increase temperature of water from 0 °C to 100 °C = $(cm\Delta T)_{water}$
 + heat to evaporate water to steam at 100 °C = $(ml)_{vaporisation\ of\ water}$

$= 2100 \times 1.00 \times [(0 - (-18)] = 37\ 800$ J
$+ 1.00 \times 3.34 \times 10^5 = 334\ 000$ J
$+ 4180 \times 1.00 \times (100-0) = 418\ 000$ J
$+ 1.00 \times 22.60 \times 10^5 = 2\ 260\ 000$ J

$= 3\ 049\ 800$ J, or 3.05×10^6 J to 3 significant figures

Cosmology

Light year

1. 3×10^8 m s^{-1}

2. (a) 8 minutes (b) 4.3 years (c) 100 000 years

3. distance

4. one light year = distance light travels in one year
   = speed × time
   = $3 \times 10^8 \times 365 \times 24 \times 60 \times 60$
   = 9.46×10^{15} m

5. The distances involved in astronomical measurements are so great that a large unit of distance is needed.

The observable universe

1. (a) A planet is a body that orbits a star, shines by reflecting the star's light and is larger than an asteroid.
   (b) A moon is a celestial body that circles a larger planet or body.
   (c) A star is a massive ball of gas that produces heat and light and is held together by its own gravity.
   (d) A solar system is a star and all the objects that travel in orbit around it.
   (e) An exoplanet is a planet that orbits a star outside of our solar system.
   (f) A galaxy is a system of millions or billions of stars, together with gas and dust, held together by gravitational attraction.
   (g) The universe is all of space and everything in it including moons, planets, stars, galaxies as well as dust and gas clouds.

2. (a) The **universe** consists of a large number of **galaxies**, such as the **Milky Way** and Andromeda, each separated by empty space.
   (b) Each **galaxy** consists of millions of **stars**, of which Proxima Centauri is the second closest to the Earth, the closest to the Earth being **the Sun**.
   (c) The Earth is one of eight **planets**, each of which orbits around the **Sun**. Such a group of heavenly bodies is known as a **solar system**.

(d) With continuing space exploration, we are discovering more and more **exoplanets** orbiting around **stars**. Over one thousand have so far been discovered. Some may have even been discovered outside our own galaxy, the **Milky Way**.

(e) Like the Earth, some of the **planets** in our own and in other **solar systems** have natural satellites which orbit around them. These satellites are called **moons**.

3. (a) The collection of all known galaxies is called the **universe**.

   (b) A **galaxy** consists of a large number of stars and solar systems.

   (c) A heavenly body which emits light and heat energy is called a **star**.

   (d) The nearest star to the Earth is **the Sun**.

   (e) Some stars, like the Sun, have several **planets** orbiting round them.

   (f) A star, together with the heavenly bodies associated with it, is collectively known as a **solar system**.

   (g) Some planets have one or more natural satellites, which are called **moons**, orbiting round them.

4. (a) the Big Bang theory

   (b) The universe originates from an 'event' at a single point. This resulted in energy/matter expanding in all directions. Hydrogen and helium atoms were first produced and all other known elements came from these two.

   (c) about 13.7 billion years ago

5. (a) Scientists have detected background microwave radiation from the early universe. It has been called cosmic microwave background radiation (CMB).

   (b) by using radio telescopes and satellites

Spectra

1. (a) A complete band of light of all frequencies and colours from red to violet with no breaks.

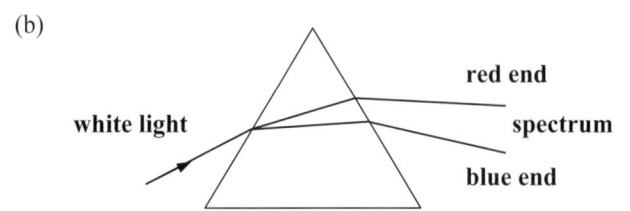

    (b)

    white light → [prism] → spectrum (red end / blue end)

2. a spectroscope

3. (a) A line spectrum consists of lines of different colours, each of which corresponds to a particular frequency of light.

    (b) Atoms of elements can emit these lines of light under certain conditions, e.g. hot gas at a low pressure, gas with an electric current through it.

    (c) The line spectrum emitted by a particular element is always the same. Each element has its own unique line spectrum. By studying the lines in the spectrum given off by a source such as a star, the elements present in the source can be identified.

4. (a) line absorbtion spectra; line emission spectra

    (b) A line absorption spectrum is a continuous spectrum with black lines in place of certain colours.
    A line emission spectrum is a series of distinct lines of different colours.

5. (a) Star 2
    (b) Star 4
    (c) Star 1
    (d) Star 3

6. (a) When light from distant stars is observed, the absorption spectra from known elements in the stars are seen to be shifted towards the red end. This effect is caused because the source of the light, the star, is moving away from the observer.

    (b) The further away a star is, the greater is the redshift. This indicates that the furthest away stars are moving away fastest and so the universe must be expanding.

Open-ended questions

By their very nature, there is a wide variety of possible answers to open-ended questions and the given mark is related to the variety and accuracy of the relevant physics in the response. There may be strengths and weaknesses in the answers and, as far as possible, the focus when marking should be on the strengths, taking account of weaknesses (errors or omissions) only where they detract from the overall answer in a significant way. The guidance below should be taken into account to determine the quality of the answer.

0 marks: The student has demonstrated no understanding of the physics that is relevant to the problem/situation.

1 mark: The student has demonstrated a limited understanding of the physics involved. The student has made some statement(s) which is/are relevant to the situation, showing that at least a little of the physics within the problem is understood.

2 marks: The student has demonstrated a reasonable understanding of the physics involved. The student makes some statement(s) which is/are relevant to the situation, showing the problem is understood.

3 marks: The maximum available mark would be awarded to a student who has demonstrated a good understanding of the physics involved. The student shows a good comprehension of the situation and has provided a logically correct answer to the question posed. This type of response might include a statement of the principles involved, a relationship or an equation, and the application of these to respond to the problem. This does not mean that the answer has to be what might be termed an "excellent' answer or a "complete" one.

Model answers to Open-ended questions

1. A light bulb converts electrical energy into heat (and light) energy when a current passes through the bulb. The filament of the light bulb is a resistor which opposes the current. A current of electricity is the movement of charges through the filament 'pushed' by the potential difference across the ends of the filament. If the bulb is removed, the circuit is broken and so the current stops, although the potential difference across the wires remains. A complete, unbroken circuit is needed for charges to flow.

2. Since the hairdryer is powered from the mains, a break in the cable would cause it to stop operating – an electrical circuit must have a complete path for the current. There could be a break that makes and breaks as the cable is flexed (sometimes called an intermittent fault), but this would not be time-related.
It is more likely that Jonny's explanation is correct. Laying the hairdryer down on soft bedclothes when it is operating could obstruct the flow of air, and this would cause the heater to overheat. The thermal switch is there to cut off the current to the heater if this happens. The thermal switch would reset after a few minutes when it cools down. This would allow the hairdryer to operate again.

3. A photovoltaic cell is a device that converts light falling on it into electrical energy. The Sun emits energy in the form of light and heat in all directions, some in the direction of the Earth. Photovoltaic cells on Earth, 150 million kilometres away, cannot affect the rate at which this radiation is emitted from the Sun.

4. The temperature of the room will increase since there is a net increase in energy in the room – the electrical energy supplying the compressor motor, which will heat up.

5. The device is called a periscope. A periscope can make use of two mirrors to reflect light or two prisms using total internal reflection of light.

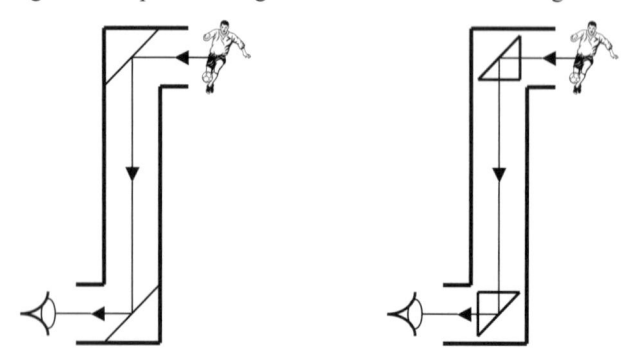

6. The torch bulb is placed at the focus of the parabolic reflector so that the light from the bulb is formed into a parallel beam.

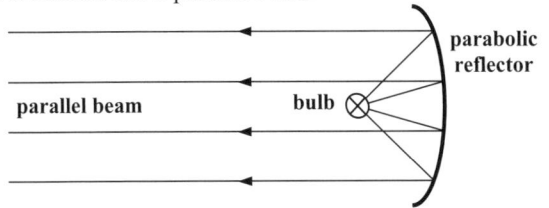

7. Although the gravitational force on a 4 kg object is twice that on a 2 kg object, both objects are in the same gravitational field. The gravitational field strength in newtons per kilogram acting on both objects is the same.
$$g = \frac{\text{weight}}{\text{mass}}$$
Both objects have the same acceleration when allowed to fall freely, and so take the same time to fall from the same height. If both objects fall from rest then they will have the same speed just before they hit the ground.
$$v = at$$
So the student is not correct.

8. Loudspeakers in the starting blocks of a sprint race ensure that all the runners hear the sound of the starting pistol at the same time. If these loudspeakers were not used, the runner nearest to the starter would hear the sound slightly earlier than the other runners and so would have a significant advantage in a short sprint race.
Runners in a marathon are each given a timing chip which they carry with them when they run. This chip electronically records when they individually cross the start and the finish lines and so all the thousands of runners do not have to start at exactly the same time for the timing to be fair.

9. Friction is a force which opposes motion. When two surfaces move over each other the force of friction generates heat.
When a match head is struck on a matchbox, the resulting friction causes heat which ignites the match. Without the friction between the soles of our shoes and the pavement, we would not be able to walk because our feet would not grip. So friction can be a friend.
However, friction can also be a problem. When moving parts of a car engine move over each other, they generate heat. The oil which is used in an engine is a lubricant which separates the moving parts slightly and this reduces the friction. Air moving past a fast moving vehicle also causes friction which slows down the vehicle and heats it up. This can be reduced by streamlining – shaping the body of the vehicle to cause the air to flow over the surface and reduce the force of friction.

10. Wearing seat belts supplies a restraining backward force to the passengers to reduce their speed in line with the reduced speed of the car. So the passengers are not hurt in the crash.
    However when the car stops suddenly, the driver who is not wearing a seat belt will not have this restraining force so will continue forward at the same speed but will *not* be "thrown forward" in relation to the ground. The newspaper article is partly correct.

11. If the friend is short-sighted, the lens will be concave. A concave lens cannot concentrate the Sun's rays since rays of light (and heat) diverge from a concave lens. A convex lens would be needed to focus the rays to start a fire.

12. The student is correct in saying that all objects in freefall from the same height have the same acceleration because they are in the same gravitational field. This means that all objects dropped from the same height have the same speed just before just before reaching the ground.
    However kinetic energy also depends on the mass of the object ($E_k = \frac{1}{2}mv^2$) so the student is not correct in saying that all objects will have the same kinetic energy just before reaching the ground.

13. On a very cold day a wooden gatepost and a metal gate will be at the same temperature, which is lower than the temperature of your hand.
    Wood is a poorer conductor of heat than metal. When you touch the metal gate, the heat from your hand is conducted away faster than when you touch the wooden gatepost.
    As a result, the metal gate feels colder than the wooden gatepost.

14. Satellites orbit the Earth because their forward speed is so great that the Earth's curved surface drops away from the satellite as much as the satellite falls towards the Earth, due to the gravitational force from the Earth.
    The period of a satellite is the time it takes for the satellite to orbit the Earth once, and period depends on the height of the satellite above the Earth.
    A geostationary satellite stays above the same point on the Earth because its height is such that its period is 24 hours – the time it takes the Earth to rotate once on its axis. This height is approximately 35,786 kilometres above sea level. So the student is not correct.

15. The light coming from the star is split into a spectrum using a prism or a diffraction grating. The spectrum is usually a continuous spectrum with absorption lines. The predominant colour of the spectrum gives an indication of the surface temperature of the star. Hotter stars are at the blue end of the spectrum; cooler stars at the red end.
    Our Sun is towards the red end of the spectrum.

16. As well as having surface liquid water, scientists believe that four other necessary conditions for an exoplanet to sustain life are that the planet orbits a stable star, is a suitable distance from its star for liquid water to exist, has a nearly circular orbit to allow constant conditions and has a suitable atmosphere.

17. The Continuously Habitable Zone (CHZ) is the region around a star where any planets could support liquid water continuously.

    Goldilocks chose the middle of three items in several instances, choosing the one that is 'just right' and rejecting the extremes. In the same way, a CHZ would have to be 'just right' and never swing between extremes. Factors that would have to be 'just right' include temperature, light level, gravitational field strength and the planet's atmosphere.